The Path

TO A BLESSED

Life

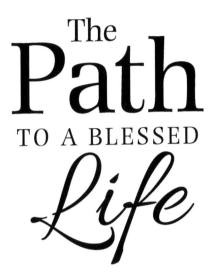

Psalm 16:11 KJV

Thou (God) wilt shew me the path of life:
in Thy presence is fulness of joy;
at Thy right hand there are pleasures for evermore.

MONICA LAN-SON

WESTBOW
PRESS®
A DIVISION OF THOMAS NELSON
& ZONDERVAN

Scripture taken from the New King James Version®. Copyright ©
1982 by Thomas Nelson. Used by permission. All rights reserved.

WestBow Press books may be ordered through booksellers or by contacting:

WestBow Press
A Division of Thomas Nelson & Zondervan
1663 Liberty Drive
Bloomington, IN 47403
www.westbowpress.com
1 (866) 928-1240

Because of the dynamic nature of the Internet, any web addresses or
links contained in this book may have changed since publication and
may no longer be valid. The views expressed in this work are solely those
of the author and do not necessarily reflect the views of the publisher,
and the publisher hereby disclaims any responsibility for them.

Any people depicted in stock imagery provided by Thinkstock are models,
and such images are being used for illustrative purposes only.
Certain stock imagery © Thinkstock.

ISBN: 978-1-5127-6722-3 (sc)
ISBN: 978-1-5127-6723-0 (hc)
ISBN: 978-1-5127-6721-6 (e)

Library of Congress Control Number: 2016920237

Print information available on the last page.

WestBow Press rev. date: 12/15/2016

First and most important of all, I am greatly thankful to the LORD God, my Creator; Christ Jesus, my Saviour; and the Holy Spirit, my Helper for this privilege work.

This book is dedicated to the person who is holding it right now.
May God bless you!
I pray this book helps you draw closer to God
and build a love relationship with Him.

Acknowlegements

A special thank you to my family and friends for believing in me, blessing me, and remembering me with God's work in your prayers.

Thank you for your love, encouragement, and support.

Also, I would like to express my appreciation to the WestBow Press's team for helping me to bring this work of God to the readers around the world.

Every one of you is eager to assist, very kind, and helpful.

I thank God for all of you.

Foreword

The Word of God is the greatest gift to mankind after the Lord Jesus Christ Himself. A devotional like this helps us draw closer to our Savior.

God often uses difficult trials and storms of life to bring His children closer to Himself. It is then that we can be used more fully for His purposes. This is how this book came to be.

Personally knowing the author, Monica, I can attest to God's working in her heart and life. She especially exhibits the joy of the Spirit.

I think you will find her insights encouraging and simple as I did. Always pointing back to the Word of Life.

May God bless this work to bring glory to His Son, Jesus Christ our Lord.

Richard J. Pidde
MD

Introduction

The Path to a Blessed Life is collection of thoughts I gained in my walk with Christ.

From fleeing the pressure in Vietnam to struggling with learning the new language of English in Canada, and through the ordeal of life-threatening cancer, I always have hope for a better future.

Although I stumbled at times and I still do, God has always upheld me. So I learn to hold on tight to God's love and His promises in the Bible to continue my walk with Him.

In my walk with the Lord, He has strengthened me and lifted me up and taught me to be strong in this world—the world that do not belong to Him and His followers.

For this reason, I want to share my life experiencing thoughts in Christ to the people in the world. I trust this is the will of God, because I have experienced His encouragement and guidance through doing His work.

May my understanding and sharing in this book helps you to have a sincere and intimate love relationship with God, set yourself apart from this world, and support you in Christ with eternal hope.

January 1

―⊙ ⊙―

Start the new year by putting God first
—Living our life God's way

Matthew 6:31, 33–34 NKJV
(Jesus said,)
Therefore do not worry, saying, 'What shall we eat?' or 'What shall
we drink?' or 'What shall we wear?'
But seek first the kingdom of God and His righteousness, and all
these things shall be added to you.
Therefore do not worry about tomorrow, for tomorrow will worry
about its own things. Sufficient for the day is its own trouble.

January 2

Our greatest desire should be to seek, obey, and honor God—to grow in love with Him.

Micah 6:8 KJV
He hath shewed thee, O man, what is good; and what doth the Lord (God) require of thee, but to do justly, and to love mercy, and to walk humbly with thy God?

January 3

When we are aligned with God in our steps, decisions, and actions, We can be confident that the end will be good.

Proverbs 16:9 KJV
A man's heart deviseth his way: but the Lord (God) directeth his steps.

Psalm 37:4 KJV
Delight thyself also in the Lord (God); and He shall give thee the desires of thine heart.

January 4

God takes care of our needs;
His salvation allows us to enter His kingdom in heaven.

Matthew 3:2 KJV
Repent ye: for the kingdom of heaven is at hand.

January 5

A blessed life is when we care not of worldly things and trust God to provide for our daily needs.

Luke 16:13 KJV
(Jesus said,)
No servant can serve two masters: for either he will hate the one, and love the other; or else he will hold to the one, and despise the other. Ye cannot serve God and mammon.

January 6

Living out faith—
Not worrying about the next step,
Nor anxious to see the distant path,
But patiently following Jesus one step at a time.

Proverbs 3:5–6 KJV
Trust in the Lord (God) with all thine heart; and lean not unto thine own understanding.
In all thy ways acknowledge Him, and He shall direct thy paths.

January 7

Be your best by living your daily life according to the teachings of the Bible.

Matthew 5:16 KJV
(Jesus said,)
Let your light so shine before men, that they may see your good works, and glorify your Father (God) which is in heaven.

January 8

The Bible is holy and inspired by God;
Every passage has its purpose and is for us to reflect on.

2 Timothy 3:16–17 KJV

All Scripture (the Bible) is given by inspiration of God, and is profitable for doctrine, for reproof, for correction, for instruction in righteousness:

That the man of God may be perfect, thoroughly furnished unto all good works.

January 9

Do not live for self.
Do not live for others.
Live for the Lord Jesus.

Romans 14:8 KJV
For whether we live, we live unto the Lord (Jesus); and whether we die, we die unto the Lord: whether we live therefore, or die, we are the Lord's.

January 10

Do not just think, but do.
Do not just plan, but act.
Live a full life in the Lord Jesus.

Psalm 37:23–24 KJV
The steps of a good man are ordered by the Lord (God): and He delighteth in his way.
Though he fall, he shall not be utterly cast down: for the Lord upholdeth him with His hand.

John 10:10b KJV
(Jesus said,)
I am come that they (mankind) might have life, and that they might have it more abundantly.

January 11

———————————— ⁊◎ ◉⊱ ————————————

Dream big and let God fit into your dream,
Because our God is the greatest God above all gods.

Ephesians 3:20 KJV
Now unto Him (God) that is able to do exceeding abundantly above all that we ask or think, according to the power that worketh in us.

January 12

~~~

Let go of your past and do not let your past limit your present opportunities.

Philippians 3:13b KJV
But this one thing I do, forgetting those things which are behind, and reaching forth unto those things which are before.

January 13

Live a life of purity before God,
And be confident of His forgiveness.

1 John 1:5b, 7 KJV
God is light, and in Him is no darkness at all.
But if we walk in the light, as He is in the light, we have fellowship one with another, and the blood of Jesus Christ His Son cleaneth us from all sin.

January 14

Confession without repentance is lack of faith and hope. Confession with repentance is full of faith and hope.

Matthew 3:8 KJV
Bring forth therefore fruits meet for repentance.

2 Corinthians 7:10 NKJV
For godly sorrow produces repentance leading to salvation, not to be regretted; but the sorrow of the world produces death.

January 15

A life with eternal hope brings lasting happiness and contentment.

Romans 6:4–5 KJV
Therefore we are buried with Him by baptism into death: that like as Christ was raised up from the dead by the glory of the Father (God), even so we also should walk in newness of life.
For if we have been planted together in the likeness of His death, we shall be also in the likeness of His resurrection.

January 16

Happiness is not just a feeling;
It is a decision we must make regardless of our circumstances.

Habakkuk 3:17–18 KJV
Although the fig tree shall not blossom, neither shall fruit be in the vines; the labor of the olive shall fail, and the fields shall yield no meat; the flock shall be cut off from the fold, and there shall be no herd in the stalls:
Yet I will rejoice in the Lord, I will joy in the God of my salvation.

January 17

━━━━━━━━━━━━━━━ ✦ ━━━━━━━━━━━━━━━

Countless things in life are unpredictable;
Trust in God who knows all and whose love for us is unchangeable.

Psalm 46:10 NKJV
Be still, and know that I am God; I will be exalted among the nations, I will be exalted in the earth!

January 18

God is love.
Do not reject God and His blessings.
Believe in Him and trust in His salvation to be blessed.

Romans 1:16a KJV
For I am not ashamed of the gospel of Christ: for it is the power of God unto salvation to everyone that believeth.

January 19

God's love can restore hope.
Godly wisdom leads to new beginning, better choices, and more ...

Psalm 33:18, 22 KJV
Behold, the eye of the Lord (God) is upon them that fear Him, upon them that hope in His mercy.
Let Thy mercy, O Lord, be upon us, according as we hope in Thee.

January 20

Do not seek earthly treasures.
Seek heavenly treasures.

Matthew 6:19–21 KJV
(Jesus said,)
Lay not up for yourselves treasures upon earth, where moth and rust doth corrupt, and where thieves break through and steal:
But lay up for yourselves treasures in heaven, where neither moth nor rust doth corrupt, and where thieves do not break through nor steal:
For where your treasure is, there will your heart be also.

January 21

Every day,
Wake up in God's presence,
Commit all things to Him,
And know that He is in control.

Proverbs 16:3 KJV
Commit thy works unto the Lord (God), and thy thoughts shall be established.

January 22

God's power is unlimited.
His will is unstoppable.

Job 9:10 KJV

(God) doeth great things past finding out; yea, and wonders without number.

Luke 18:27 KJV

(Jesus said,)
The things which are impossible with men are possible with God.

January 23

Put God's Word into practice in your daily life to guard against falling into temptation.

Ephesians 6:13 KJV
Wherefore take unto you the whole armor of God, that ye may be able to withstand in the evil day, and having done all, to stand.

January 24

———— ✺◎ ◎✺ ————

When you are faced with temptations,
Satan is attacking your faith in Christ.

Matthew 26:41 KJV
(Jesus said,)
Watch and pray, that ye enter not into temptation: the spirit indeed is willing, but the flesh is weak.

January 25

———— ⚘ ⚘ ————

Every temptation is an opportunity to strengthen your faith, Knowing that Jesus has already overcome Satan.

1 John 3:10 KJV
In this the children of God are manifest, and the children of the devil: whosoever doth not righteousness is not of God, neither he that loveth not his brother (and sister).

January 26

God has His timing in all things;
Therefore, stand firm and hold on to your faith.

Ecclesiastes 3:1 KJV
To every thing there is a season, and a time to every purpose under the heaven.

Luke 21:19 KJV
(Jesus said,)
In your patience possess ye your souls.

January 27

In good or bad times,
We can find joy in God's presence.

2 Corinthians 6:10 KJV
As sorrowful, yet always rejoicing; as poor, yet making many rich; as having nothing, and yet possessing all things.

January 28

~@ @~

Jesus is with us always as we go through different seasons and times in our journey of life.

Matthew 28:20 KJV

(Jesus said,)

Teaching them to observe all things whatsoever I have commanded you: and, lo, I am with you always, even unto the end of the world. Amen.

January 29

Salvation is not only a promise of eternity with God,
But it is also a daily experience of grace in our relationship with Him.

Matthew 6:10 KJV
(Jesus said,)
Thy (God's) kingdom come. Thy will be done in earth, as it is in heaven.

January 30

Life with Jesus is a blessed one;
We find purpose, meaning, and joy in Him.

John 14:6a KJV
(Jesus said,)
I am the way, the truth, and the life.

January 31

Jesus Christ is the eternal Lord.
His love and mercy are everlasting.
His truth endures to all generations.

Revelation 22:13 KJV
(Jesus said,)
I am Alpha and Omega, the beginning and the end, the first and the last.

February 1

The cross is the symbol of the greatest commandment:
- Vertical relationship between people and God.
- Horizontal relationship between people.

Mark 12:30–31 KJV
(Jesus said,)
Thou shalt love the Lord thy God with all thy heart, and with all thy soul, and with all thy mind, and with all thy strength: this is the first commandment.
And the second is like, namely this, Thou shalt love thy neighbour as thyself. there is none other commandment greater than these.

February 2

―――――― ⁊◎ ◎ᔆ ――――――

From beginning to end,
God's desire is not for us to be religious,
But for us to have a relationship with Him.

1 John 4:16b KJV
God is love; and he that dwelleth in love dwelleth in God, and God in him.

February 3

Love God,
Not the religious activities.

Hosea 6:6 KJV
For I (God) desired mercy, and not sacrifice; and the knowledge of God more than burnt offerings.

February 4

❧ ◊❧

Do not turn God into a religion.
Believe in Christ not as a religion.

2 Corinthians 5:18–19a, 20b–21 KJV
All things are of God, who hath reconciled us to Himself by Jesus
Christ, and hath given to us the ministry of reconciliation;
To wit, that God was in Christ, reconciling the world unto Himself,
not imputing their trespasses unto them …
… Be ye reconciled to God.
For He (God) hath made Him (Christ) to be sin for us, who knew
no sin; that we might be made the righteousness of God in Him.

February 5

When we allow anyone or anything to be above God,
We create an idol for ourselves.

Exodus 20:3–6 KJV
Thou shalt have no other gods before Me.

Thou shalt not make unto thee any graven image, or any likeness of any thing that is in heaven above, or that is in the earth beneath, or that is in the water under the earth:

Thou shalt not bow down thyself to them, nor serve them: for I the Lord thy God am a jealous God, visiting the iniquity of the fathers upon the children unto the third and fourth generation of them that hate Me;

And shewing mercy unto thousands of them that love Me, and keep My commandments.

February 6

⚜

Human beings are spiritual refugees;
Only in Jesus can we find sanctuary for our souls.

John 15:9–11 KJV
(Jesus said,)
As the Father (God) hath loved Me, so have I loved you: continue
ye in My love.
If ye keep My commandments, ye shall abide in My love; even as I
have kept My Father's commandments, and abide in His love.
These things have I spoken unto you, that My joy might remain in
you, and that your joy might be full.

February 7

God's people are blessed to bless others.
Let your blessings overflow!

2 Corinthians 9:8 KJV
God is able to make all grace abound toward you; that ye, always having all sufficiency in all things may abound to every good work.

February 8

Everyone is gifted with words of encouragement.
In times of need, be generous to lift others up with your words.

1 Thessalonians 5:11 KJV
Wherefore comfort yourselves together, and edify one another, even as also ye do.

February 9

We all have weaknesses and faults,
So bear with each other and forgive one another when things go wrong.
Exhortation should be done with love and kindness to build each other up.

Colossians 3:12–13 NKJV
Therefore, as the elect of God, holy and beloved, put on tender mercies, kindness, humility, meekness, longsuffering; bearing with one another, and forgiving one another, if anyone has a complaint against another; even as Christ forgave you, so you also must do.

February 10

Kind words given at the right moment can make someone's day.

Proverbs 12:25 NKJV
Anxiety in the heart of man causes depression,
But a good word makes it glad.

February 11

It is only when we dwell in God's love
That we learn to love one another genuinely.

1 John 4:19 KJV
We love Him (God), because He first loved us.

1 Peter 1:22 NKJV
Since you have purified your souls in obeying the truth through the (Holy) Spirit in sincere love of the brethren, love one another fervently with a pure heart.

February 12

❧ ⊙~

Love, faith, forgiveness, and kindness is the foundation of family.

Proverbs 10:12b KJV
Love covereth all sins.

1 John 4:18 KJV
There is no fear in love; but perfect love casteth out fear: because fear hath torment. He that feareth is not made perfect in love.

February 13

In a family,
Not only parents can bless their children,
But children can also bless their parents.

Psalm 115:13 KJV
He (God) will bless them that fear the Lord, both small and great.

February 14

Successful parenting starts with focusing on God and making Him the center of all we do.

Parents seeking to have good relationships with their children must put God first in their family.

Deuteronomy 12:28 KJV
Observe and hear all these words which I command thee, that it may go well with thee, and with thy children after thee for ever, when thou doest that which is good and right in the sight of the Lord thy God.

February 15

―――――――――――――― ✺◎ ◎✺ ――――――――――――――

Young children carry no responsibilities,
Yet often want to help.
Older children neglect their responsibilities
And tend not to help.
Adults are those who take responsibilities
And show signs of maturity.

1 Corinthians 13:4–8a NKJV

Love suffers long and is kind; love does not envy; love does not
parade itself, is not puffed up; does not behave rudely, does not seek
its own, is not provoked, thinks no evil; does not rejoice in iniquity,
but rejoices in the truth; bears all things, believes all things, hopes
all things, endures all things.
Love never fails.

February 16

Marriage is a husband and wife
Living life together,
Sharing life together,
And finishing life together strong.

Ephesians 5:31, 33 KJV
... Shall a man leave his father and mother, and shall be joined unto his wife, and they two shall be one flesh.
Nevertheless let every one of you in particular so love his wife even as himself; and the wife see that she reverence her husband.

February 17

Bring your children to Jesus
That they may receive His blessings,
Because He loves them.

Luke 18:16b–17 NKJV
(Jesus said,)
Let the little children come to Me, and do not forbid them; for of such is the kingdom of God.
Assuredly, I say to you, whoever does not receive the kingdom of God as a little child will by no means enter it.

February 18

There is one thing we must keep in mind:
God's love for us is never changing—endless love.

Ephesians 1:3–4 KJV
Blessed be the God and Father of our Lord Jesus Christ, who hath blessed us with all spiritual blessings in heavenly places in Christ: According as He hath chosen us in Him before the foundation of the world, that we should be holy and without blame before Him in love.

February 19

Love without doubt.
Live without fear.
Trust never falters.

Psalm 13:5 KJV
I have trusted in Thy (God's) mercy; my heart shall rejoice in Thy
salvation.

February 20

God declared His love to humanity.
He showed us His love through His action.

1 John 4:9 KJV
In this was manifested the love of God toward us, because that God sent His only begotten Son (Jesus Christ) into the world, that we might live through Him.

February 21

Mankind should respond to God's love by loving God more than anything in the world.

Nehemiah 1:5 NKJV
I pray, Lord God of heaven, O great and awesome God, You who keep Your covenant and mercy with those who love You and observe Your commandments.

February 22

Abide in God's love.
The world will come to past;
Only God's love lasts forever.

Psalm 143:8 KJV
Cause me to hear Thy (God's) lovingkindness in the morning; for in Thee do I trust: cause me to know the way wherein I should walk; for I lift up my soul unto Thee.

February 23

Jesus told us to love God,
Love one another,
Love our neighbors,
And love our enemies.

1 John 4:7–8 KJV
Beloved, let us love one another: for love is of God; and every one that loveth is born of God, and knoweth God.
He that loveth not knoweth not God; for God is love.

February 24

Love our neighbors would be difficult if we do not acknowledge them.

Love our enemies requires us to go the extra mile.

Matthew 5:43–45a KJV
(Jesus said,)
Ye have heard that it hath been said, Thou shalt love thy neighbour, and hate thine enemy.

But I say unto you, Love your enemies, bless them that curse you, do good to them that hate you, and pray for them which despitefully use you, and persecute you;

That ye may be the children of your Father (God) which is in heaven.

February 25

Who are our neighbors?

They are people whom we know, often see, or come to our mind in our daily lives: our family, relatives, friends, schoolmates, and co-workers.

They also include people we do not know whom God has placed in our lives.

Romans 15:2 KJV

Let every one of us please his neighbour for his good to edification.

February 26

If we love God,
We must love those God loves.

Matthew 5:45b–46a, 48 KJV
(Jesus said,)
He (God) maketh His sun to rise on the evil and on the good, and sendeth rain on the just and on the unjust.
For if ye love them which love you, what reward have ye?
Be ye therefore perfect, even as your Father (God) which is in heaven is perfect.

February 27

It is easy to love people whom we like,
But learn to love those who are unlovable,
Because our human nature is unlovable-sinner.

Romans 3:22–24 KJV
Even the righteousness of God which is by faith of Jesus Christ
unto all and upon all them that believe: for there is no difference:
For all have sinned, and come short of the glory of God;
Being justified freely by His grace through the redemption that is
in Christ Jesus.

February 28

❧ ⌘

Express your love.
The action of love is powerful.

1 John 3:18 KJV
... Let us not love in word, neither in tongue; but in deed and in truth.

Philemon 1:7a KJV
For we have great joy and consolation in thy love.

February 29

When we love God, obey Him, and follow Jesus' example,
The world will become a better place.

1 John 4:12 KJV
No man hath seen God at any time. If we love one another, God
dwelleth in us, and His love is perfected in us.

March 1

∙◉ ◉∙

Why is the truth so hard to believe?

- God's love and man's sin.
- God's covenant and man's pride.
- God's initiative and man's passiveness.
- God never forsakes man;

But man falls away from God, loves the world, ignores conscience, and deceives oneself.

John 3:16 KJV

(Jesus said,)

For God so loved the world, that He gave His only begotten Son (Jesus Christ), that whosoever believeth in Him should not perish, but have everlasting life.

March 2

Man's sinfulness is seen by his and her selfishness.
God's righteousness is shown through Christ's selflessness.

Romans 5:7–8 NKJV
For scarcely for a righteous man will one die; yet perhaps for a good man someone would even dare to die.
But God demonstrates His own love toward us, in that while we were still sinners, Christ died for us.

March 3

We made a mess (our sin), and Jesus cleaned it up (He died) for us;
Never did Jesus expect us to clean up our own mess.
Be grateful to our Savior, our Lord Jesus Christ!

James 1:21 NKJV
Therefore lay aside all filthiness and overflow of wickedness, and receive with meekness the implanted word which is able to save your souls.

March 4

Our minds are troubled by doubts,
And our hearts are overwhelmed with worries;
Jesus knows and understands us completely,
Yet He loves us unconditionally.

Romans 5:6 KJV
For when we were yet without strength, in due time Christ died for the ungodly.

March 5

God's grace is free, unconditional, and priceless.

Romans 3:24–26 KJV
Being justified freely by His (God's) grace through the redemption that is in Christ Jesus:
Whom God hath set forth to be a propitiation through faith in His blood, to declare His righteousness for the remission of sins that are past, through the forbearance of God;
To declare, I say, at this time His righteousness: that He might be just, and the justifier of him which believeth in Jesus.

March 6

God is our provider, protector, defender, and deliverer.

Psalm 62:6–7 KJV
He only is my rock and my salvation: He is my defence; I shall not be moved.
In God is my salvation and my glory: the rock of my strength, and my refuge, is in God.

March 7

We need not feel insignificant;
God of the universe loves us regardless.

Lamentations 3:22–23 KJV
It is of the Lord's (God's) mercies that we are not consumed, because His compassions fail not.
They are new every morning: great is Thy faithfulness.

March 8

Law is to observe our conduct.
Grace is rooted in God's kindness.

Romans 6:14 KJV
For sin shall not have dominion over you: for ye are not under the law, but under grace.

March 9

Salvation is God's grace;
It cannot be gained by good works.

Romans 11:6 KJV
And if by grace, then is it no more of works: otherwise grace is no more grace. But if it be of works, then it is no more grace: otherwise work is no more work.

March 10

We are saved not because of our good works;
We are saved so as to do good works.

Ephesians 2:10 KJV
For we are His (God's) workmanship, created in Christ Jesus unto good works, which God hath before ordained that we should walk in them.

March 11

───────────────── ⁊◎ ◎⁊ ─────────────────

Without having a close relationship with God,
Our worship and service are in vain.

Isaiah 29:13 KJV
Wherefore the Lord (God) said, Forasmuch as this people draw
near Me with their mouth, and with their lips do honour Me, but
have removed their heart far from Me, and their fear toward Me is
taught by the precept of men.

March 12

Our focus and enthusiasm is central to the relationship we have with Christ.

Colossians 2:6–7 KJV
As ye have therefore received Christ Jesus the Lord, so walk ye in Him:
Rooted and built up in Him, and stablished in the faith, as ye have been taught, abounding therein with thanksgiving.

March 13

Christians should work as a team to serve God in the same mindset; There is no need to compete with each other.

Romans 15:5–6 KJV
Now the God of patience and consolation grant you to be likeminded one toward another according to Christ Jesus:
That ye may with one mind and one mouth glorify God, even the Father of our Lord Jesus Christ.

March 14

God accomplishes in us,
Not only what is beneficial for us
But also what is good for us.

Romans 8:28 KJV
We know that all things work together for good to them that love
God, to them who are the called according to His purpose.

March 15

꩜ ꩜

When we bring ourselves into alignment with God,
We will find joy in life.

Psalm 68:3 KJV
But let the righteous be glad; let them rejoice before God: yea, let them exceedingly rejoice.

March 16

⚜

Humble yourself in the love, forgiveness, and presence of God;
And you will find freedom, peace, and hope.

Psalm 86:5 KJV
For Thou, Lord (God), art good, and ready to forgive; and plenteous
in mercy unto all them that call upon Thee.

March 17

～ ❧ ☙ ～

The Bible helps us understand God's love by His salvation given to us through His Son Jesus Christ.

1 Timothy 2:3–6 KJV
For this is good and acceptable in the sight of God our Saviour;
Who will have all men to be saved, and to come unto the knowledge of the truth.
For there is one God, and one Mediator between God and men, the man Christ Jesus;
Who gave Himself a ransom for all, to be testified in due time.

March 18

Salvation is a gift from God;
It cannot be earned.

Ephesians 2:8–9 KJV
For by grace are ye saved through faith; and that not of yourselves:
it is the gift of God:
Not of works, lest any man should boast.

March 19

Jesus Christ's salvation is given freely to both the rich and the poor.

Romans 10:13 KJV
For whosoever shall call upon the name of the Lord (Jesus Christ) shall be saved.

March 20

Earthly blessings are precious to us,
But what God deems as precious are not limited to earthly blessings.

Psalm 37:18 KJV
The Lord (God) knoweth the days of the upright: and their inheritance shall be for ever.

March 21

Wealth is not measured by how much we have,
But how we do with what we have that matters.

Proverbs 8:18 KJV
Riches and honour are with me (wisdom); yea, durable riches and righteousness.

March 22

Money can buy things in the world,
But it cannot buy our entry into heaven.

James 5:1–3 KJV
Go to now, ye rich men, weep and howl for your miseries that shall
come upon you.
Your riches are corrupted, and your garments are motheaten.
Your gold and silver is cankered; and the rust of them shall be a
witness against you, and shall eat your flesh as it were fire. Ye have
heaped treasure together for the last days.

March 23

~~~

Jesus is the only way into heaven.
Believe in Him and He will grant you eternal life.

Romans 10:9–10 KJV
That if thou shalt confess with thy mouth the Lord Jesus, and shalt believe in thine heart that God hath raised Him from the dead, thou shalt be saved.
For with the heart man believeth unto righteousness; and with the mouth confession is made unto salvation.

March 24

Sin separates mankind from God.
Jesus' love and sacrifice on the cross reconciles us with God—our Creator.

Colossians 1:19–20 KJV
For it pleased the Father (God) that in Him (Jesus) should all fulness dwell;
And, having made peace through the blood of His cross, by Him to reconcile all things unto Himself; by Him, I say, whether they be things in earth, or things in heaven.

March 25

God's love is completely manifested on the cross.
Jesus' salvation on the cross gives us Hope.

1 John 4:9–10 KJV
In this was manifested the love of God toward us, because that God
sent His only begotten Son (Jesus Christ) into the world, that we
might live through Him.
Herein is love, not that we loved God, but that He loved us, and
sent His Son to be the propitiation for our sins.

March 26

God blesses us through Jesus Christ who died on the cross for us. Jesus set an example of obeying God and honoring God's will.

Luke 22:42 KJV

(Jesus said,)

Father (God), if Thou be willing, remove this cup from Me: nevertheless not My will, but Thine, be done.

March 27

When we do not think about things in the world
And do not care what the world thinks of us,
We become more like our Lord Jesus Christ.

1 John 2:15 KJV
Love not the world, neither the things that are in the world. If any man love the world, the love of the Father (God) is not in him.

March 28

Accept Christ to be your personal savior,
And the Holy Spirit will come and reside in your heart.

Romans 8:9–10 KJV
But ye are not in the flesh, but in the Spirit, if so be that the Spirit of God dwell in you. Now if any man have not the Spirit of Christ, he is none of His.
And if Christ be in you, the body is dead because of sin; but the Spirit is life because of righteousness.

March 29

Follow your heart—allow the Holy Spirit inside your heart to guide you.

1 Corinthians 2:12 KJV
Now we have received, not the spirit of the world, but the spirit which is of God; that we might know the things that are freely given to us of God.

March 30

We all have a wish list and are waiting for miracles to happen; Christ's love on the Cross is the greatest miracle.

Galatians 3:26 KJV
For ye are all the children of God by faith in Christ Jesus.

March 31

Faith enables miracles to happen;
Believe in the Lord Jesus Christ and have faith in Him.

Matthew 9:29b KJV
(Jesus) saying,
According to your faith be it unto you.

April 1

God's Word has the power to change lives.

Isaiah 40:28–29 KJV

Hast thou not known? hast thou not heard, that the everlasting God, the Lord, the Creator of the ends of the earth, fainteth not, neither is weary? there is no searching of His understanding.
He giveth power to the faint; and to them that have no might He increaseth strength.

April 2

God's Word provides wisdom
And positive outlook on life.

Isaiah 33:6 KJV
Wisdom and knowledge shall be the stability of thy times, and strength of salvation: the fear of the Lord (God) is His treasure.

April 3

God's Word helps us to have an eternal perspective
And gives us the true meaning of life.
His Word is our power.

Psalm 16:11 KJV
Thou (God) wilt shew me the path of life: in Thy presence is fulness
of joy; at Thy right hand there are pleasures for evermore.

April 4

───────── ✺◉ ◎✺ ─────────

We often find ourselves complaining moments in life that do not go our way,
Rather than focusing on the good things our heavenly Father (God) has given us.

Psalm 90:12 KJV
So (God) teach us to number our days, that we may apply our hearts unto wisdom.

April 5

Stop feeling sorry for yourself;
Pull yourself together and get out of self-pity.

Psalm 138:3 KJV
In the day when I cried Thou (God) answeredst me, and strengthenedst me with strength in my soul.

April 6

~⊚ ⊚~

Every day,
Replace doubt, anxiety, and negative thoughts
With trust, stillness, and positive thoughts in God's Word.

Luke 12:25–28 KJV
(Jesus said,)
Which of you with taking thought can add to his stature one cubit?
If ye then be not able to do that thing which is least, why take ye
thought for the rest?
Consider the lilies how they grow: they toil not, they spin not …
If then God so clothe the grass … how much more will He
clothe you.

April 7

Let go of things you do not have the answers to,
And trust Jesus completely and simply follow Him.

John 12:46 KJV
(Jesus said,)
I am come a light into the world, that whosoever believeth on Me should not abide in darkness.

April 8

ᕙ◎ ◎ᕛ

No matter what baggage you are carrying
And whatever spiritual goals you have yet to achieve,
Entrust everything into God's hands.

Psalm 55:22 KJV
Cast thy burden upon the Lord (God), and He shall sustain thee:
He shall never suffer the righteous to be moved.

April 9

There are times when we fall short of our expectations,
And times when we brim with confidence:
In all times, humble ourselves before God!

Psalm 33:21 KJV
For our heart shall rejoice in Him (God), because we have trusted
in His holy name.

April 10

When people are up at the peak,
Satan tells them to be proud,
But Jesus teaches them to be humble.

When people are down to the pit,
Satan causes them to be frustrated and discouraged,
But Jesus strengthens them and gives them hope.

Proverbs 18:12 KJV
Before destruction the heart of man is haughty, and before honour
is humility.

April 11

ꙮ

Weeping with those who weep may be easier;
Perhaps we are better than they are.
Rejoicing with those who rejoice may be harder;
Perhaps they are better than we are.
Always humble ourselves
As we share in others weeping and rejoicing.

Romans 12:15–16a KJV
Rejoice with them that do rejoice, and weep with them that weep.
Be of the same mind one toward another.

April 12

Everyone likes to compare.
Comparison can lead to competition.
Competition is good only if it sharpens one another.
Comparison can also lead to jealousy.
Jealousy brings on negativity and discouragement.
We all have our gifts from God.
Keep our focus on God, please God and not people.
Do our best with the gifts God gave us.

1 Peter 4:10 KJV
As every man hath received the gift, even so minister the same one to another, as good stewards of the manifold grace of God.

April 13

You will experience true happiness
When you are no longer jealous or envious of others.

Proverbs 14:30 KJV
A sound heart is the life of the flesh: but envy the rottenness of the bones.

April 14

$\mathbf{Y}$ou will experience true peace
When you no longer compare and bicker.

James 3:16–18 NKJV
For where envy and self-seeking exist, confusion and every evil thing are there.
But the wisdom that is from above is first pure, then peaceable, gentle, willing to yield, full of mercy and good fruits, without partiality, and without hypocrisy.
Now the fruit of righteousness is sown in peace by those who make peace.

April 15

Know in your heart God's Word,
Not what the world is telling you.

John 15:19a KJV

(Jesus said,)

If ye were of the world, the world would love his own: but because ye are not of the world, but I have chosen you out of the world.

April 16

When a person is not ready to receive,
It is of no value to offer advice.

1 Corinthians 1:18 KJV
For the preaching of the cross is to them that perish foolishness;
but unto us which are saved it is the power of God.

April 17

When we insist on our viewpoint and think we are better than others,
We are blinded by pride and not exercising our love.
We think we are helping, but we are not.

Proverbs 18:2 NKJV
A fool hath no delight in understanding,
But in expressing his own heart.

April 18

❧ ❧

Words are powerful:

- What to say and how to say it.
- What not to say and when to stay silent.

Words have the power to build up and to tear down.

Matthew 15:11 KJV
(Jesus said,)
Not that which goeth into the mouth defileth a man; but that which cometh out of the mouth, this defileth a man.

April 19

If we cannot speak kind words,
We must not speak.
When we do speak,
We must speak with graciousness rather than accusation or negativity.
Our words must glorify God and not exalt ourselves.

Colossians 4:6 KJV
Let your speech be always with grace, seasoned with salt, that ye
may know how ye ought to answer every man.

April 20

***

Our words and deeds reflect our hearts.
We please God when we show His love in what we say and do.

Colossians 3:16a–17 KJV
Let the word of Christ dwell in you richly in all wisdom …
And whatsoever ye do in word or deed, do all in the name of the
Lord Jesus, giving thanks to God and the Father by Him.

April 21

Communicate with love and humility—
Focus not on self,
Nor on earthly things,
But on heavenly things.

Romans 15:7 KJV
Wherefore receive ye one another, as Christ also received us to the glory of God.

April 22

When there is disagreement,
No one has to win or lose.

Proverbs 15:1, 18 KJV
A soft answer turneth away wrath: but grievous words stir up anger.
A wrathful man stirreth up strife: but he that is slow to anger
appeaseth strife.

April 23

Nobody comes out of an argument winning,
But only broken relationship.
Let Jesus be our answer to resolving all arguments.

Philippians 2:4–6 KJV
Look not every man on his own things, but every man also on the things of others.
Let this mind be in you, which was also in Christ Jesus:
Who, being in the form of God, thought it not robbery to be equal with God.

April 24

Do not live by the comments of the world;
Live by the assurance of God's love.

2 Thessalonians 2:16–17 KJV
Now our Lord Jesus Christ Himself, and God, even our Father, which hath loved us, and hath given us everlasting consolation and good hope through grace,
Comfort your hearts, and stablish you in every good word and work.

April 25

Embrace the truth.
Value who you are.
You are a wonderful creation of God.

Psalm 139:14 KJV
I will praise thee (God); for I am fearfully and wonderfully made: marvellous are Thy works; and that my soul knoweth right well.

April 26

God can bring out the best in you and lead you into new and wonderful things.

Psalm 147:5 KJV
Great is our Lord (God), and of great power: His understanding is infinite.

April 27

※◎ ◎※

Practice a healthy living,
Balance your body and soul.

1 Thessalonians 5:23 KJV
The very God of peace sanctify you wholly; and I pray God your whole spirit and soul and body be preserved blameless unto the coming of our Lord Jesus Christ.

April 28

Change begins in your mind.
Let God transform you by changing the way you think.

Psalm 25:9 KJV
The meek will He (God) guide in judgment: and the meek will He
teach His way.

April 29

Satan wants us to think we are helpless.
But God is our help.
Use God's Word to counter the devil's lies.

Psalm 62:1–2 KJV
Truly my soul waiteth upon God: from Him cometh my salvation. He only is my rock and my salvation; He is my defence; I shall not be greatly moved.

April 30

Do not be discouraged and fall into the habit of laziness. Live by faith and serve God wholeheartedly to receive your reward in heaven.

Romans 12:11 KJV
Not slothful in business; fervent in spirit; serving the Lord (God).

Hebrews 6:12 KJV
That ye be not slothful, but followers of them who through faith and patience inherit the promises.

May 1

Jesus was clear in telling His disciples what they would expect from this world
When He spoke to them ...

John 16:33b KJV
(Jesus said,)
... In the world ye shall have tribulation: but be of good cheer; I have overcome the world.

May 2

For followers of Christ,
The world is a great place for spiritual development whether in good or bad times.

Ecclesiastes 7:14 KJV
In the day of prosperity be joyful, but in the day of adversity consider: God also hath set the one over against the other, to the end that man should find nothing after him.

May 3

It is easy for us to see God in times of our favor.
But can we see God in times of our trouble?

Nahum 1:7 KJV
The Lord (God) is good, a strong hold in the day of trouble; and He knoweth them that trust in Him.

May 4

God uses both blessings and trials
To challenge us and change us for the better.
He can change us into whom He has created us to be.

James 1:12 KJV
Blessed is the man that endureth temptation: for when he is tried, he shall receive the crown of life, which the Lord (God) hath promised to them that love Him.

May 5

If you only want a temporary change,
Work on the outside—your external behaviors.
If you desire a permanent change,
Work on the inside—your internal thoughts.

Matthew 7:24, 26 KJV
(Jesus said,)
Therefore whosoever heareth these sayings of Mine, and doeth them, I will liken him unto a wise man, which built his house upon a rock.

And every one that heareth these sayings of Mine, and doeth them not, shall be likened unto a foolish man, which built his house upon the sand.

May 6

Reality check—am I putting my faith in God, but still living as if everything was up to me?

We ought to align our behavior with our belief.
We ought to live our lives in accordance with God's Word.

Job 27:6 KJV
My righteousness I hold fast, and will not let it go: my heart shall not reproach me so long as I live.

May 7

When you give up something, it makes room for God to bring new things into your life.

Do not rush to fill your time or emotional space with activities.

Devote yourself to prayer, and pay attention to what God brings into your life.

Psalm 90:17 KJV
Let the beauty of the Lord our God be upon us: and establish Thou the work of our hands upon us; yea, the work of our hands establish Thou it.

May 8

Satan's plan is to trick us into rejecting God and pursuing our own ideas.
We must believe God is in charge, not in human intervention.
Always follow the truth in the Bible.

Psalm 25:5 KJV
Lead me in Thy truth, and teach me: for Thou art the God of my salvation; on Thee do I wait all the day.

May 9

Do not fall prey to the values of the world;
You will miss what God could have done through you.
At the same time, you would have wasted your entire life.

Matthew 16:26 KJV
(Jesus said,)
For what is a man profited, if he shall gain the whole world, and lose his own soul? or what shall a man give in exchange for his soul?

May 10

We must not let Satan's lies take away the joy in our hearts.
In Christ, we have the power to overcome the devil.
Let us praise God and enjoy His protection and provision.

Philippians 4:4 KJV
Rejoice in the Lord (Jesus Christ) always: and again I say, Rejoice.

May 11

Do not fear Satan.
Fear the LORD God.

Psalm 140:13 KJV
Surely the righteous shall give thanks unto Thy (God's) name: the upright shall dwell in Thy presence.

May 12

─────────────────── ✺ ◉ ✺ ───────────────────

God's love abides in us.
His grace sets us free through Jesus' salvation.

John 8:31b–32 KJV
(Jesus said,)
If ye continue in My word, then are ye My disciples indeed;
And ye shall know the truth, and the truth shall make you free.

May 13

Your life is a result of your choices.
The decision is yours: live a lifeless or a vibrant life.

Psalm 118:24 KJV
This is the day which the Lord (God) hath made; we will rejoice and be glad in it.

May 14

Living a vibrant life full of faith will bring you fullness of Joy.

Hebrews 11:6 KJV
But without faith it is impossible to please Him: for he that cometh to God must believe that He is, and that He is a rewarder of them that diligently seek Him.

May 15

When you lack confidence,
Jesus can increase your faith.

Mark 9:24b NKJV
Lord (Jesus), I believe; help my unbelief!

May 16

Stand firm in your faith,
Not based on your feelings;
Otherwise you are bound to fall.

Romans 5:1–4 KJV
Therefore being justified by faith, we have peace with God through
our Lord Jesus Christ:
By whom also we have access by faith into this grace wherein we
stand, and rejoice in hope of the glory of God.
And not only so, but we glory in tribulations also: knowing
that tribulation worketh patience; and patience, experience; and
experience, hope.

May 17

Do not think of difficult times as setbacks;
Think of them as setup times
As God prepares us for great times ahead.

Hebrews 12:10–11 KJV

... Chastened us ... He (God) for our profit, that we might be partakers of His holiness.

Now no chastening for the present seemeth to be joyous, but grievous: nevertheless afterward it yieldeth the peaceable fruit of righteousness unto them which are exercised thereby.

May 18

No matter how difficult things may become
And we do not understand what God is doing,
Trust God to make all things good for us.

Jeremiah 17:7 KJV
Blessed is the man that trusteth in the Lord (God), and whose hope
the Lord is.

May 19

Pains and difficulties are part of life;
They make us to be more like our Lord Jesus Christ.

Hebrews 12:2 KJV
Looking unto Jesus the author and finisher of our faith; who for the joy that was set before Him endured the cross, despising the shame, and is set down at the right hand of the throne of God.

May 20

Your words matter.
Tell the next generation what God has done for you.

Luke 1:46–47, 50 KJV
... My soul doth magnify the Lord (God),
And my spirit hath rejoiced in God my Saviour.
And His mercy is on them that fear Him from generation to generation.

May 21

Do not let your children be influenced by the world.
Teach your children the truth in the Bible while they are young and with you.

Psalm 119:9 NKJV
How can a young man cleanse his way?
By taking heed according to Your (God's) word.

May 22

Teach your children not to love the world;
Teach them to love God and be close to Him.

Deuteronomy 6:7 KJV
Thou shalt teach them (the Lord God's words) diligently unto thy children, and shalt talk of them when thou sittest in thine house, and when thou walkest by the way, and when thou liest down, and when thou risest up.

May 23

Teach your children the love of the world will send them far away from God.
Teach your children the love of Christ will keep them far away from Satan.

Romans 8:5 KJV
For they that are after the flesh do mind the things of the flesh; but they that are after the (Holy) Spirit the things of the Spirit.

May 24

If you bless your children with the love of the world,
It will lead them into the gates of death.
If you bless your children with the love of Christ,
It will lead them into the gate of heaven.

Proverbs 19:18 NKJV
Chasten your son (children) while there is hope,
And do not set your heart on his destruction.

Romans 8:6 KJV
For to be carnally minded is death; but to be spiritually minded is
life and peace.

May 25

Do not focus on the temporary things in the world.
Focus on things in heaven which bring eternal blessings.

Galatians 6:8 KJV

For he that soweth to his flesh shall of the flesh reap corruption; but he that soweth to the (Holy) Spirit shall of the Spirit reap life everlasting.

May 26

༜ↂ ☺ↄ

Train your children to read the Bible and know the truth which can set them free.

Proverbs 14:27 KJV
The fear of the Lord (God) is a fountain of life, to depart from the snares of death.

May 27

Satan's work is to destroy our love and relationships with God and with one another.

We need to be vigilant:

Love God and love one another to defeat the devil.

James 4:7–8a KJV

Submit yourselves therefore to God. Resist the devil, and he will flee from you.

Draw nigh to God, and He will draw nigh to you.

May 28

The devil likes to twist our words.
Use positive words to express your love.

1 Corinthians 13:6 KJV
(Love) Rejoiceth not in iniquity, but rejoiceth in the truth.

May 29

People interpret our words differently.
Always use constructive words to deliver your messages.

Psalm 85:10 KJV
Mercy and truth are met together; righteousness and peace have kissed each other.

May 30

Body language is powerful.
Use body language to express love.

1 Corinthians 13:13 NKJV
Now abide faith, hope, love, these three; but the greatest of these
is love.

May 31

There are times when those we love disappoint us,
And times when they bring us great joy:
In all times, always have hope!

Psalm 62:5 KJV
My soul, wait thou only upon God; for my expectation is from Him.

June 1

Happy Father's Day to our heavenly Father (God)!
Thank You for Your great love!
Please help us love You and pass Your love on to a thousand generations.

Deuteronomy 7:9 KJV
Know therefore that the Lord thy God, He is God, the faithful God, which keepeth covenant and mercy with them that love Him and keep His commandments to a thousand generations.

June 2

〜◎ ◎〜

Through the blood of Christ Jesus our Lord,
We are redeemed by God's grace
And changed by His love;
Hence, we live by faith
And wait in hope for our Lord's return.

Ephesians 2:13 KJV
But now in Christ Jesus ye who sometimes were far off are made nigh by the blood of Christ.

June 3

When people see us,
God desires them to see Jesus in us.

John 14:11–12 KJV
(Jesus said,)
Believe Me that I am in the Father (God), and the Father in Me: or else believe Me for the very works' sake.
Verily, verily, I say unto you, He that believeth on Me, the works that I do shall he do also; and greater works than these shall he do …

June 4

Live an upright life in this upside-down world.

Titus 2:11–14 KJV
For the grace of God that bringeth salvation hath appeared to all men,
Teaching us that, denying ungodliness and worldly lusts, we should live soberly, righteously, and godly, in this present world;
Looking for that blessed hope, and the glorious appearing of the great God and our Saviour Jesus Christ;
Who gave Himself for us, that He might redeem us from all iniquity, and purify unto Himself a peculiar people, zealous of good works.

June 5

Live a life that challenges the norm of this world
And reclaims our culture in Christ:
Do not blend in, stand apart from the crowd instead.

Philippians 3:20–21 NKJV
For our citizenship is in heaven, from which we also eagerly wait
for the Savior, the Lord Jesus Christ, who will transform our lowly
body that it may be conform to His glorious body, according to the
working by which He is able even to subdue all things to Himself.

June 6

Trusting the Lord God
Or relying on yourself
Determines where your life will lead you.

Isaiah 55:8–9 KJV
For My thoughts are not your thoughts, neither are your ways My ways, saith the Lord (God).
For as the heavens are higher than the earth, so are My ways higher than your ways, and My thoughts than your thoughts.

June 7

~~~

God has made us totally capable of living a life full of love, forgiveness, and peace through Christ.

2 Corinthians 13:11 KJV
Be perfect, be of good comfort, be of one mind, live in peace; and the God of love and peace shall be with you.

June 8

Honor God and bless others:
Build healthy relationships and fulfill your responsibilities.

Philippians 2:13 KJV
For it is God which worketh in you both to will and to do of His good pleasure.

June 9

〰️

When you doubt your ability in the face of challenges,
Remember you are capable because God gives you strength.

Ephesians 1:17, 19–20 KJV
That the God of our Lord Jesus Christ, the Father of glory, may give unto you the spirit of wisdom and revelation in the knowledge of Him:
And what is the exceeding greatness of His power to us-ward who believe, according to the working of His mighty power,
Which He wrought in Christ when He raised Him from the dead, and set Him at His own right hand in the heavenly places.

June 10

God does not ask us to do things beyond our capabilities;
He only asks us to do things within our abilities.

Matthew 25:15, 23 KJV
Unto one (a servant) he (a master) gave five talents, to another two,
and to another one; to every man according to his several ability ...
His lord (the master) said unto him, Well done, good and faithful
servant; thou hast been faithful over a few things, I will make thee
ruler over many things: enter thou into the joy of thy lord.

June 11

~❦ ❧~

Even if it seems like God does not care about your situations,
Keep on praying and trusting Him,
Because we cannot comprehend His way.

Psalm 23:4 KJV
Yea, though I walk through the valley of the shadow of death, I will fear no evil: for Thou (God) art with me; Thy rod and Thy staff they comfort me.

June 12

Allow God to remove all the obstacles along the way of your path and open up a new road for you.

Isaiah 57:14 NKJV
(The Lord God said,)
Heap it up! Heap it up!
Prepare the way,
Take the stumbling block out of the way of My people.

June 13

When God closes a door,
No one can open it;
When God opens a door,
No one can close it.

Revelation 3:7b KJV
He (Jesus Christ) that is holy, He that is true ... He that openeth, and no man shutteth; and shutteth, and no man openeth.

June 14

Read God's Word.
Know God's will.
Live out God's priorities, not the priorities of the world.

John 17:16–17 KJV
(Jesus said,)
They (Jesus' disciples) are not of the world, even as I am not of the world.
Sanctify them through Thy (God's) truth: Thy word is truth.

June 15

See the world through God's perspective.
Revolve your life around what God sees as important.

1 John 2:17 KJV
The world passeth away, and the lust thereof: but he that doeth the will of God abideth for ever.

June 16

Make time to connect with God,
And let the power of His Spirit strengthens and renews you.

Ephesians 3:16–17, 19 KJV
That He (God) would grant you, according to the riches of His glory, to be strengthened with might by His Spirit in the inner man; That Christ may dwell in your hearts by faith; that ye, being rooted and grounded in love ...
And to know the love of Christ, which passeth knowledge, that ye might be filled with all the fulness of God.

June 17

❧ ❧

The greatest gift parents can give to their children is to teach them to fear God and build a love relationship with Him.

Psalm 103:11 KJV
For as the heaven is high above the earth, so great is His (God's) mercy toward them that fear Him.

June 18

God commands children to honor their parents;
Do not disregard this commandment as it comes with a promise.

Ephesians 6:1–3 KJV
Children, obey your parents in the Lord (God): for this is right.
Honour thy father and mother; which is the first commandment with promise;
That it may be well with thee, and thou mayest live long on the earth.

June 19

❧ ⊚ ☙

God gives parents the responsibilities to bring up their children according to His instructions in the Bible.

Psalm 34:11–12 KJV
Come, ye children, hearken unto me: I will teach you the fear of the Lord (God).
What man is he that desireth life, and loveth many days, that he may see good?

June 20

Parents should tell their young children about God's love,
And they will grow up loving and honoring God into their old age.

Proverbs 22:6 KJV
Train up a child in the way he should go: and when he is old, he will not depart from it.

June 21

Teach your children to fear God.
Instruct your children to obey God.
Pray for your children to love God and walk in His will.

Psalm 31:19 KJV
Oh how great is Thy (God's) goodness, which Thou hast laid up for them that fear Thee; which Thou hast wrought for them that trust in Thee before the sons of men!

June 22

Besides teaching your children everything according to God's Word,
It is essential for parents to live a godly life in God's presence as a role model for your children.

Proverbs 20:7 KJV
The just man walketh in his integrity: his children are blessed after him.

June 23

⚜ ⚜

If you want your children to love God,
Let them feel you loving God.

1 John 5:3 NKJV
For this is the love of God, that we keep His commandments. And
His commandments are not burdensome.

June 24

If you want your children to fear God,
Let them see you fearing God.

Psalm 34:9 KJV
O fear the Lord (God), ye His saints: for there is no want to them
that fear Him.

June 25

If you want your children to follow God's desire,
Let them witness you following God's desire.

Psalm 40:8 KJV
I delight to do Thy will, O my God: yea, Thy law is within my heart.

June 26

Teach your children not only with words but also with actions. Actions are more powerful than words.

James 2:20, 24 KJV
But wilt thou know, O vain man, that faith without works is dead? Ye see then how that by works a man is justified, and not by faith only.

June 27

A father who desires to be more like the Lord Jesus pleases God and brings blessings to his children.

Ephesians 4:23–24 KJV
Be renewed in the spirit of your mind;
And that ye put on the new man, which after God is created in righteousness and true holiness.

June 28

Be patient,
Because God is patient with us.
With the help of the Holy Spirit,
We wait patiently for our eternal hope.

Romans 15:4 KJV
For whatsoever things were written aforetime were written for our learning, that we through patience and comfort of the scriptures might have hope.

June 29

～⊙ ⊙～

Keep your faith and be strengthened by grace in Christ Jesus to finish life well.

Psalm 73:25–26 KJV
Whom have I in heaven but Thee (God)? and there is none upon earth that I desire beside Thee.
My flesh and my heart faileth: but God is the strength of my heart, and my portion for ever.

June 30

Our work on earth can never be done,
But God's work is already complete.
Trust in God's power to find rest for our souls.

Hebrews 4:10–11 KJV
For he that is entered into His (God's) rest, he also hath ceased from his own works, as God did from His.
Let us labour therefore to enter into that rest, lest any man fall after the same example of unbelief.

July 1

Circumstances will challenge our faith;
Focus on what God is doing in our heart and not on the external situations.

Zechariah 4:6b KJV
Not by might, nor by power, but by My spirit, saith the Lord (God) of hosts.

July 2

When doubt threatens your faith,
Be still in God's presence and embrace His promises.

Hebrews 10:23 KJV
Let us hold fast the profession of our faith without wavering; (for
He (God) is faithful that promised.)

July 3

Do not allow the devil to use the insecurities of your past to rob you from living confidently as a forgiven child of God.

Ephesians 3:11–12 KJV
According to the eternal purpose which He (God) purposed in Christ Jesus our Lord:
In whom we have boldness and access with confidence by the faith of Him.

July 4

Bring yourself close to God in prayer.

Hebrews 13:6 KJV
So that we may boldly say, The Lord (God) is my helper, and I will not fear what man shall do unto me.

July 5

Do not pray as if you are having a monologue with yourself. Pray to God like you are having a dialog with a loved one.

Matthew 6:6 KJV

(Jesus said,)

But thou, when thou prayest, enter into thy closet, and when thou hast shut thy door, pray to thy Father (God) which is in secret; and thy Father which seeth in secret shall reward thee openly.

July 6

※◎ ◎※

Prayer is not about self-talk, self-condemnation, self-fixing, or self-obsession.

Romans 8:1 KJV
There is therefore now no condemnation to them which are in Christ Jesus, who walk not after the flesh, but after the (Holy) Spirit.

July 7

Do not pray out of obligation.
Do not pray under the pressure of guilt.
Do not pray for God to fulfill your desires.
Rather, pray because you are your heavenly Father's (God's) child.

Luke 3:21b, 22b NKJV
… While He (Jesus) prayed, the heaven was opened.
… And a voice came from heaven which said,
"You are My beloved Son; in You I am well pleased."

July 8

Let your list of praises to God be longer than your list of petitions.

Matthew 6:7–8 KJV

(Jesus said,)

But when ye pray, use not vain repetitions, as the heathen do: for they think that they shall be heard for their much speaking.

Be not ye therefore like unto them: for your Father (God) knoweth what things ye have need of, before ye ask Him.

July 9

~⊚ ⊚~

A rich relationship with Jesus is much more precious than presenting Him a list of requests.

1 John 5:12 KJV
He that hath the Son (Jesus) hath life; and he that hath not the Son of God hath not life.

July 10

Do not be proud in well-expressed prayer.
Do not feel embarrassed in incoherent prayer.

1 John 3:20–21 KJV
For if our heart condemn us, God is greater than our heart, and knoweth all things.
Beloved, if our heart condemn us not, then have we confidence toward God.

July 11

Prayer is being with God.

Mark 1:35 KJV
In the morning, rising up a great while before day, He (Jesus) went out, and departed into a solitary place, and there prayed.

July 12

Prayer is powerful when we pray in the name of the Lord Jesus Christ.

John 14:13 KJV
(Jesus said,)
Whatsoever ye shall ask in My name, that will I do, that the Father (God) may be glorified in the Son (Jesus).

July 13

Our prayer is pleasing to God when we pray according to His will.

John 9:31 KJV
Now we know that God heareth not sinners: but if any man be a worshipper of God, and doeth His will, him He heareth.

July 14

———————————— ✺◎ ◎✺ ————————————

God hears our prayer when we obey God and bear no grudges against others.

Mark 11:25–26 NKJV
(Jesus said,)
Whenever you stand praying, if you have anything against anyone, forgive him, that your Father (God) in heaven may also forgive you your trespasses.
But if you do not forgive, neither will your Father in heaven forgive your trespasses.

July 15

The power of prayer.

The power to pray.

No authority can stop us from praying to our God, our heavenly Father.

In Jesus' name we pray. Amen.

Romans 8:31b KJV

If God be for us, who can be against us?

July 16

─────────────── ✺◎ ◎✺ ───────────────

Study God's Word.
Be sensitive to the Holy Spirit's guidance.
Be faithful in prayer in Jesus' name.

Jude 1:20–21 KJV
But ye, beloved, building up yourselves on your most holy faith,
praying in the Holy Ghost (Spirit),
Keep yourselves in the love of God, looking for the mercy of our
Lord Jesus Christ unto eternal life.

July 17

Make your daily schedule revolves around things that are important in eternity.

2 Corinthians 4:18 KJV
While we look not at the things which are seen, but at the things which are not seen: for the things which are seen are temporal; but the things which are not seen are eternal.

July 18

Worship God for who He is and what He has done for us.
Although we can express our love for God in many forms and in
different environments,
It is the heart behind the actions that matters most to God.

Proverbs 21:2 KJV
Every way of a man is right in his own eyes: but the Lord (God)
pondereth the hearts.

July 19

We go to church, not because we like some of the people there. Likewise, we do not stop going to church, simply because some of the people there don't like us.

We go to church because of Jesus, and not because of people.

Philippians 2:4–5 KJV

Look not every man on his own things, but every man also on the things of others.

Let this mind be in you, which was also in Christ Jesus.

July 20

If you work very hard to please God and are only concerned about appearing godly,
Then you have totally missed God.

Psalm 51:10 KJV
Create in me a clean heart, O God; and renew a right spirit within me.

July 21

Worshiping and serving God is not about showcasing your talents.
Abandon your performance-based relationship,
And establish a genuine relationship with God.

Jonah 2:7 KJV
When my soul fainted within me I remembered the Lord (God): and my prayer came in unto Thee, into Thine holy temple.

July 22

Serve the Lord your God.
Do not serve your ministry.

Luke 4:8b KJV
(Jesus said,)
For it is written, Thou shalt worship the Lord thy God, and Him only shalt thou serve.

July 23

Loving God is utmost.
Serving God is an outcome.

Mark 12:33 KJV
To love Him (God) with all the heart, and with all the understanding, and with all the soul, and with all the strength, and to love his neighbour as himself, is more than all whole burnt offerings and sacrifices.

July 24

Do not do things to win people's admiration.
Do all things to win God's heart.

Galatians 1:10 KJV
For do I now persuade men, or God? or do I seek to please men? for
if I yet pleased men, I should not be the servant of Christ.

July 25

People today consider being busy as being important.
Do not let your busy schedule rob you of your time with God.
Prioritize your schedule and focus on God.

Psalm 65:8 NKJV
They also who dwell in the farthest parts are afraid at Your (God's) signs:
You make the outgoings of the morning and evening to rejoice.

July 26

Allow interruptions into your busy life;
Take time to be with God to reflect, meditate, pray, and praise Him.

Exodus 15:2 NKJV
The Lord is my strength and song,
And He has become my salvation;
He is my God, and I will praise Him …

July 27

⦿ ⦿

Whenever you cannot think of anything to say to God, listen to Him with your heart.

Romans 8:26 KJV
The (Holy) Spirit also helpeth our infirmities: for we know not what we should pray for as we ought: but the Spirit itself maketh intercession for us with groanings which cannot be uttered.

July 28

A good relationship is a two-way communication.
To have a good relationship with God,
We do not just pray (we talk and God listens),
But we also need to read the Bible (God talks and we listen).

Luke 11:9 KJV
(Jesus said,)
I say unto you, Ask, and it shall be given you; seek, and ye shall find;
knock, and it shall be opened unto you.

July 29

Prayer without faith is futile.

James 1:6–8 KJV
But let him ask in faith, nothing wavering. For he that wavereth is like a wave of the sea driven with the wind and tossed.
For let not that man think that he shall receive any thing of the Lord (God).
A double minded man is unstable in all his ways.

July 30

Faith leads us to inherit God's promises.
Fear hinders us to receive God's blessings.

2 Peter 3:9 KJV
The Lord (God) is not slack concerning His promise, as some men count slackness; but is longsuffering to us-ward, not willing that any should perish, but that all should come to repentance.

July 31

Take a leap in your faith,
And you will experience an abundant life in Christ.

1 Timothy 1:14 KJV
The grace of our Lord (God) was exceeding abundant with faith and love which is in Christ Jesus.

August 1

Good things are stumbling blocks to great things.
Set your heart on heavenly things,
And do not doubt but wait in expectation.

1 John 2:15–17 KJV
Love not the world, neither the things that are in the world. If any man love the world, the love of the Father (God) is not in him. For all that is in the world, the lust of the flesh, and the lust of the eyes, and the pride of life, is not of the Father, but is of the world. And the world passeth away, and the lust thereof: but he that doeth the will of God abideth for ever.

August 2

In today's social media frenzy,
We tend to be influenced by what we see.
We must not merely show ourselves.
We need to let others see Jesus in us.

John 8:12b KJV
(Jesus said,)
I am the light of the world: he that followeth Me shall not walk in darkness, but shall have the light of life.

August 3

Many people want to be saved,
But do not want to be changed.
They want to believe in Christ,
But do not want to surrender to Him.

Galatians 6:7–8 KJV
Be not deceived; God is not mocked: for whatsoever a man soweth, that shall he also reap.
For he that soweth to his flesh shall of the flesh reap corruption; but he that soweth to the (Holy) Spirit shall of the Spirit reap life everlasting.

August 4

To many people are busy making a comfortable life on earth,
That they neglect their need to prepare for an eternal life in heaven.
Reprioritize life and spend time with God.

John 12:25 KJV
(Jesus said,)
He that loveth his life shall lose it; and he that hateth his life in this
world shall keep it unto life eternal.

August 5

In today's fast-paced culture,
It is easy to be obsessed with getting everything done.
Do not let a busy life rob you from having quality time with Jesus.

John 15:5 KJV
(Jesus said,)
I am the vine, ye are the branches: He that abideth in Me, and I in him, the same bringeth forth much fruit: for without Me ye can do nothing.

August 6

$$\ast\!\!\text{@} \;\; \text{@}\!\!\ast$$

Each day,
Pushing aside your seemingly never-ending-to-do list
Instead of pushing aside your time with God.

Psalm 92:2 KJV
To shew forth Thy (God) lovingkindness in the morning, and Thy faithfulness every night.

August 7

Having boundaries makes life better.

Matthew 12:35 KJV
(Jesus said,)
A good man out of the good treasure of the heart bringeth forth good things: and an evil man out of the evil treasure bringeth forth evil things.

August 8

~⊙ ⊙~

Self-centered:
- Focusing on self.
- Relying on the power of self to show off self.

Christ-centered:
- Focusing on Christ.
- Relying on the power of Christ to reveal Christ.

1 Corinthians 1:25 KJV
Because the foolishness of God is wiser than men; and the weakness of God is stronger than men.

August 9

Self-focused and effort-driven
Puts unrealistic expectations on self and others.
Christ-focused and love-driven
Puts realistic expectations on self and others.

Luke 6:43 KJV
(Jesus said,)
For a good tree bringeth not forth corrupt fruit; neither doth a corrupt tree bring forth good fruit.

August 10

~~~~~~

Pursue righteousness,
Not self-righteousness.

John 5:30 KJV
(Jesus said,)
I can of Mine own self do nothing: as I hear, I judge: and My judgment is just; because I seek not Mine own will, but the will of the Father (God) which hath sent Me.

August 11

The self-righteous will see only oneself.
The pure in heart will see God.

Hebrews 10:22a KJV
Let us draw near (to God) with a true heart in full assurance of faith …

Matthew 5:8 KJV
(Jesus said,)
Blessed are the pure in heart: for they shall see God.

August 12

───────────── ⚭ ─────────────

In today's materialistic world,
Worship God and live with gratitude.

Deuteronomy 11:16 KJV
Take heed to yourselves, that your heart be not deceived, and ye turn aside, and serve other gods, and worship them.

August 13

God is not a controlling God.
He gives us free will to make our own choices.

Romans 6:23 KJV
For the wages of sin is death; but the gift of God is eternal life through Jesus Christ our Lord.

August 14

Be careful in exercising your free will.
Your choices come with consequences.

Psalm 9:7 KJV
But the Lord (God) shall endure for ever: He hath prepared His throne for judgment.

August 15

Do not blame God for the consequences of your bad choices.
Come before Him in humility,
And make the right choices according to the teachings of the Bible.

John 6:27 NKJV
(Jesus said,)
Do not labor for the food which perishes, but for the food which
endures to everlasting life, which the Son of Man (Jesus) will give
you, because God the Father has set His seal on Him.

August 16

God wants us to obey Him,
Not for His own sake but for ours.

John 6:40 KJV
(Jesus said,)
This is the will of Him (God) that sent Me, that every one which seeth the Son (Jesus), and believeth on Him, may have everlasting life: and I will raise him up at the last day.

August 17

Obeying God does not deprive us from enjoying the things in the world.
Before God created mankind,
He created all the things in the world for us to enjoy.

Genesis 1:1 KJV
In the beginning God created the heaven and the earth.

Psalm 84:11–12 KJV
For the Lord God is a sun and shield: the Lord will give grace and glory: no good thing will He withhold from them that walk uprightly. O Lord of hosts, blessed is the man that trusteth in Thee.

August 18

Obey God and follow Christ.
Live a life that honors God.

Romans 2:6–8 KJV
Who (God) will render to every man according to his deeds:
To them who by patient continuance in well doing seek for glory and honour and immortality, eternal life:
But unto them that are contentious, and do not obey the truth, but obey unrighteousness, indignation and wrath.

August 19

Learn to have faith in prayer.
Learn to trust and let go.
Learn to wait in peace and hope with joy.

Psalm 86:2–4 KJV
Preserve my soul; for I am holy: O Thou my God, save Thy servant that trusteth in Thee.
Be merciful unto me, O Lord: for I cry unto Thee daily.
Rejoice the soul of Thy servant: for unto Thee, O Lord, do I lift up my soul.

August 20

$\mathcal{R}$

Faith grows through trials.
Joy comes with endurance and patience in trials.

Romans 12:12 KJV
Rejoicing in hope; patient in tribulation; continuing instant in prayer.

August 21

While waiting for your prayer to be answered,
Allow God to prepare and equip you.
And when God answers your prayer,
You are ready to glorify Him.

Hebrews 13:20–21 KJV
Now the God of peace, that brought again from the dead our Lord
Jesus … through the blood of the everlasting covenant,
Make you perfect in every good work to do His will, working in
you that which is wellpleasing in His sight, through Jesus Christ; to
whom be glory for ever and ever. Amen.

August 22

Do not stress over a problem
When you cannot do anything to solve it.
When you can do something to solve a problem,
Think through it and take actions.

2 Corinthians 3:5 KJV
Not that we are sufficient of ourselves to think any thing as of
ourselves; but our sufficiency is of God.

August 23

Lift your eyes above your circumstances.
Trust and rely on God's faithfulness.

1 Peter 4:19 KJV
Wherefore let them that suffer according to the will of God commit the keeping of their souls to Him in well doing, as unto a faithful Creator.

August 24

The problem of humanity lies not on the things surround us but in the thoughts within us.

Ezekiel 36:26 KJV
(The LORD God said,)
A new heart also will I give you, and a new spirit will I put within you: and I will take away the stony heart out of your flesh, and I will give you an heart of flesh.

August 25

The root of many problems is due to unmet expectations;
If not properly dealt with,
They lead to anger and bitterness.

Genesis 50:20a KJV
But as for you, ye thought evil against me; but God meant it unto good.

August 26

※◎ ◎※

Instead of standing up for oneself,
Kneel down and pray for others.

Psalm 17:2 NKJV
Let my vindication come from Your (God's) presence;
Let Your eyes look on the things that are upright.

August 27

If you do not agree with any brothers or sisters in Christ,
Pray for them
And pray for yourself;
Ask God to help each of you to see things from God's perspective.

Hebrews 12:14 KJV
Follow peace with all men, and holiness, without which no man shall see the Lord (God).

August 28

Jesus calls His sheep by name.
Even if we do not know the names of any brothers or sisters in Christ,
A simple 'hi' with a warm smile
Can show our love in Christ and make their day pleasant.

John 10:3, 11, 14 KJV
… He calleth his own sheep by name …
(Jesus said,)
I am the good shepherd: the good shepherd giveth His life for the sheep.
I am the good shepherd, and know My sheep, and am known of Mine.

August 29

───────────────── ⁊◎ ◎ℛ ─────────────────

Do not serve alone.

It is a blessing to serve with brothers and sisters in Christ.

Philippians 2:1–2 NKJV

Therefore if there is any consolation in Christ, if any comfort of love, if any fellowship of the (Holy) Spirit, if any affection and mercy,

… Being like-minded, having the same love, being of one accord, of one mind.

August 30

We should work together to proclaim God's kingdom. Proclaiming God's kingdom is not a one-person job.

Ephesians 3:6 KJV

That the Gentiles should be fellowheirs, and of the same body, and partakers of His (God's) promise in Christ by the gospel.

August 31

The wicked fear the coming of God's judgment day.
The faithful look forward to the return of Christ with joy.

2 Corinthians 5:10 KJV
For we must all appear before the judgment seat of Christ; that every one may receive the things done in his body, according to that he hath done, whether it be good or bad.

September 1

Shape your mind
—From self-esteem to God-esteem

Proverbs 15:33 KJV
The fear of the Lord (God) is the instruction of wisdom; and before
honour is humility.

September 2

We can acquire the knowledge in the Bible,
But only with the help of the Holy Spirit can we obtain the wisdom in it.

1 Corinthians 2:9–10 KJV
But as it is written, Eye hath not seen, nor ear heard, neither have entered into the heart of man, the things which God hath prepared for them that love Him.
But God hath revealed them unto us by His Spirit: for the Spirit searcheth all things, yea, the deep things of God.

September 3

Knowledge is
Self-learned, proud, harsh, hostile, worldly, and look down on others.

Wisdom is
God-given, humble, gentle, peace, godly, and look up to Christ.

Proverbs 11:2 KJV
When pride cometh, then cometh shame: but with the lowly is wisdom.

September 4

Pride takes us away from God;
It leads us to trust in our own strength—become proud and self-sufficient.
Humility draws us near to God;
It requires us to trust in God—depend on His strength and be thankful.

Psalm 20:7 KJV
Some trust in chariots, and some in horses: but we will remember the name of the Lord our God.

September 5

~⊚ ⊚~

A fool's godlessness is blinded by his pride.
A wise person sees God with his humility.

Proverbs 10:8 KJV
The wise in heart will receive commandments: but a prating fool shall fall.

September 6

Turn away from trusting the unreliable self.
Turn to the reliable and resurrected Christ.

Galatians 5:24–25 KJV
They that are Christ's have crucified the flesh with the affections and lusts.
If we live in the (Holy) Spirit, let us also walk in the Spirit.

September 7

Our choices in life should reflect the character of Christ and draw people to Him.

Matthew 5:13a, 14a KJV
(Jesus said,)
Ye are the salt of the earth.
Ye are the light of the world.

September 8

***

Treat everyone as you would treat yourself,
And you won't play down your relationship with them.

Luke 6:31 KJV
(Jesus said,)
As ye would that men should do to you, do ye also to them likewise.

September 9

~⊚ ⊚~

Do not show partiality.
Be even more sensitive to sensitive people.
Regard everyone with Christ's love.

Philippians 2:3–5 KJV
Let nothing be done through strife or vainglory; but in lowliness of mind let each esteem other better than themselves.
Look not every man on his own things, but every man also on the things of others.
Let this mind be in you, which was also in Christ Jesus.

September 10

Serving God is not only doing your best at school, at work, at church, and in the community;
Taking care of loved ones at home is also a service to God.
Serving God is never trivial nor insignificant.
It is a privilege to serve God wherever He puts us.

1 Corinthians12:4 KJV
Now there are diversities of gifts, but the same (Holy) Spirit.

September 11

━━━━━━━━━━━━━━━━ ❧ ☙ ━━━━━━━━━━━━━━━━

Take on work in accordance with your God-given gifts.
Do not assume the work of others in which you are not gifted.

Romans 12:6a KJV
Having then gifts differing according to the grace that is given to us.

September 12

~⊚ ⊚~

Do not conceal your weaknesses and flaws;
Trust and let God use them for His good purpose.

1 Corinthians 1:27 NKJV
But God has chosen the foolish things of the world to put to shame
the wise, and God has chosen the weak things of the world to put
to shame the things which are mighty.

September 13

───────────── ❧ ❦ ─────────────

You cannot control what others say,
But you can control how you react.
Guard your heart!
Surrender to Christ, not to Satan.

Philippians 4:7 KJV
The peace of God, which passeth all understanding, shall keep your
hearts and minds through Christ Jesus.

7

September 14

―――――――――――――――――――― ೧◎ ◎ೞ ――――――――――――――――――――

Compromise may not stand for what is right.

Psalm 119:66 KJV
Teach me good judgment and knowledge: for I have believed Thy (God's) commandments.

September 15

ᘓ◎ ◎ᕹ

Take off the lens of the world.
Put on the lens of God.

John 1:14 NKJV
The Word (God) became flesh, and dwelt among us, and we beheld
His glory, the glory as of the only begotten of the Father (God), full
of grace and truth.

September 16

Do not test or challenge God.
Do what is right according to His Word which pleases Him.

Jeremiah 17:10 NKJV
I, the Lord (God), search the heart,
I test the mind,
Even to give every man according to his ways,
According to the fruit of his doings.

September 17

It is one thing to know the teachings of the Bible;
It is quite another to live it.

James 2: 26 KJV
For as the body without the spirit is dead, so faith without works is dead also.

September 18

Do not pollute your heart with worldly desires;
Ask God for a clean heart eager for His desire.

3 John 1:11 KJV
Beloved, follow not that which is evil, but that which is good. He
that doeth good is of God: but he that doeth evil hath not seen God.

September 19

Confess your sins to God.

Ask Him to give you a new heart.

And live a new life reflecting the goodness of your new heart.

Ephesians 4:22–24 KJV

That ye put off concerning the former conversation the old man, which is corrupt according to the deceitful lusts;

And be renewed in the spirit of your mind;

And that ye put on the new man, which after God is created in righteousness and true holiness.

September 20

꩜ ☞

Destructive behavior belongs to Satan—to tear down.
Constructive behavior belongs to Christ—to build up.

1 Corinthians 10:23 NKJV
All things are lawful for me, but not all things are helpful; all things
are lawful for me, but not all things edify.

September 21

Greed blinds our hearts.
Share in heavenly inheritances, not in earthly possessions.

Luke 12:15 KJV
(Jesus said,)
Take heed, and beware of covetousness: for a man's life consisteth
not in the abundance of the things which he possesseth.

September 22

Jealousy blinds our eyes.
Desire blessings of Christ, not of the world.

Colossians 3:1–2 KJV
If ye then be risen with Christ, seek those things which are above, where Christ sitteth on the right hand of God.
Set your affection on things above, not on things on the earth.

September 23

━━━━━━━━━━━━━━ ⁊◎ ◎⁊ ━━━━━━━━━━━━━━

Do not bury yourself in unrealistic desires;
Walk with the Lord Jesus Christ in the light.

Psalm 139:23–24 KJV
Search me, O God, and know my heart: try me, and know my thoughts:
And see if there be any wicked way in me, and lead me in the way
everlasting.

September 24

The struggle of life can be our blessings
When we humbly draw near to Christ.

1 Peter 3:13–15 KJV
Who is he that will harm you, if ye be followers of that which is good?
But and if ye suffer for righteousness' sake, happy are ye: and be not afraid of their terror, neither be troubled;
But sanctify the Lord God in your hearts: and be ready always to give an answer to every man that asketh you a reason of the hope that is in you with meekness and fear.

September 25

Godis perfect who does no mistake in creating you;
Trust and submit yourself to God to enjoy peace and inherit eternal life.

Psalm 139:13, 16 NKJV
For You (God) formed my inward parts;
You covered me in my mother's womb.
Your eyes saw my substance, being yet unformed.
And in your book they all were written,
The day fashioned for me,
When as yet there were none of them.

September 26

God's law allows us to know our sins;
Only God's grace can free us from our sins and eternal punishment.

Ephesians 1:7 KJV
In whom (Christ) we have redemption through His blood, the forgiveness of sins, according to the riches of His grace.

September 27

Do not weigh yourself down with God's law.
God's intent is not to crush us;
Rather, it is Satan's attempt to fail us.

Matthew 11:28–30 KJV
(Jesus said,)
Come unto Me, all ye that labour and are heavy laden, and I will give you rest.
Take My yoke upon you, and learn of Me; for I am meek and lowly in heart: and ye shall find rest unto your souls.
For My yoke is easy, and My burden is light.

September 28

❧ ❦

Do not believe in Satan's lies which magnify your weaknesses. Do not hide your weaknesses from God who gives you strength.

2 Corinthians 12:9a KJV
(Jesus said,)
My grace is sufficient for thee: for my strength is made perfect in weakness.

September 29

Do not believe in Satan's lies which make us feel guilty;
But look upon our Lord Jesus whose love for us has covered all our guilt.

Colossians 1:13–14 KJV
Who (God) hath delivered us from the power of darkness, and hath translated us into the kingdom of His dear Son (Jesus):
In whom we have redemption through His blood, even the forgiveness of sins.

September 30

Satan is the father of all lies.

Do not let Satan deceive you.

Turn to Jesus and trust in Him who already has victory over Satan.

1 John 5:4–5 KJV

For whatsoever is born of God overcometh the world: and this is the victory that overcometh the world, even our faith.

Who is he that overcometh the world, but he that believeth that Jesus is the Son of God?

October 1

Happiness comes from your heart.
A grateful heart brings joy to your soul.
Think about what you have, not what you do not have.
Always be thankful!

1 Chronicles 16:34 KJV
O give thanks unto the Lord (God); for He is good; for His mercy endureth for ever.

October 2

A greedy person only sees what others have;
A grateful person always sees what God has blessed him or her with.

Psalm 37:16–17 KJV
A little that a righteous man hath is better than the riches of many wicked.
For the arms of the wicked shall be broken: but the Lord (God) upholdeth the righteous.

October 3

Replace bitterness with gratefulness in your daily life,
And you will be amazed to see God's love and His blessings.

Romans 8:35, 38–39b KJV
Who shall separate us from the love of Christ? shall tribulation, or distress, or persecution, or famine, or nakedness, or peril, or sword? For I am persuaded, that neither death, nor life ... nor things present, nor things to come,
... Shall be able to separate us from the love of God, which is in Christ Jesus our Lord.

October 4

~ ❧ ☙ ~

Live with a thankful heart and experience true happiness beyond your circumstances.

Philippians 4:11b KJV
For I have learned, in whatsoever state I am, therewith to be content.

October 5

～◎ ◎～

Believe in Jesus.
Do not let your circumstances control your emotions.
Let peace and joy dwell in your heart.

Romans 15:13 KJV
Now the God of hope fill you with all joy and peace in believing,
that ye may abound in hope, through the power of the Holy Ghost
(Spirit).

October 6

───────────── ✦ ✦ ─────────────

Do not borrow from tomorrow and burden yourself today.

Philippians 4:6 KJV
Be careful for nothing; but in every thing by prayer and supplication with thanksgiving let your requests be made known unto God.

October 7

Be thankful!
Live in God's love.
Enjoy Jesus' gift of peace.

Jude 1:1b–2 KJV
To them that are sanctified by God the Father, and preserved in Jesus Christ, and called:
Mercy unto you, and peace, and love, be multiplied.

October 8

There are times when we have a lot,
And times when we have little:
In all times, give thanks!

1 Thessalonians 5:16–18 KJV
Rejoice evermore.
Pray without ceasing.
In every thing give thanks: for this is the will of God in Christ Jesus
concerning you.

October 9

Write a list of all things you are grateful for,
Include the big and the small things.

Psalm 34:8 KJV
O taste and see that the Lord (God) is good: blessed is the man that
trusteth in Him.

October 10

Develop an attitude of gratefulness can open our mind and uplift our mood.

Hebrews 12:28 KJV
Wherefore we receiving a kingdom which cannot be moved, let us have grace, whereby we may serve God acceptably with reverence and godly fear.

October 11

A content person sees the hardship of the poor;
A discontent person sees only the joy of the rich.

Proverbs 28:6 KJV
Better is the poor that walketh in his uprightness, than he that is
perverse in his ways, though he be rich.

October 12

Do what God wants you to do,
And have what God wants you to have.

Proverbs 22:1–2 KJV
A good name is rather to be chosen than great riches, and loving favour rather than silver and gold.
The rich and poor meet together: the Lord (God) is the maker of them all.

October 13

Love the giver of gifts more than the gifts.

Matthew 7:11 KJV
(Jesus said,)
If ye then, being evil, know how to give good gifts unto your children, how much more shall your Father (God) which is in heaven give good things to them that ask Him?

October 14

―――――――――――― ❧ ☙ ――――――――――――

Life is not about complaining and cursing,
But thanksgiving and praising.

Psalm 100:4 KJV
Enter into His (God's) gates with thanksgiving, and into His courts
with praise: be thankful unto Him, and bless His name.

October 15

Satan deliberately puts thoughts that are in conflict with God's Word in our minds;

We must purposely dwell on thoughts that are honoring God to guard our hearts from Satan's evil thoughts.

2 Corinthians 5:9 KJV

Wherefore we labour, that, whether present or absent, we may be accepted of Him (God).

October 16

All wrongdoing is sin.
Sin brings death.
Only through Christ can we be given eternal life.

Romans 5:21 KJV
That as sin hath reigned unto death, even so might grace reign through righteousness unto eternal life by Jesus Christ our Lord.

October 17

―――――――――――――――❧◉◉❧―――――――――――――――

Do not believe Satan's lies who feeds us guilt.
But trust in the Lord God who gives us assurance of His love.

Isaiah 54:10 KJV
For the mountains shall depart, and the hills be removed; but My kindness shall not depart from thee, neither shall the covenant of My peace be removed, saith the Lord (God) that hath mercy on thee.

October 18

When trials and hardships hit,
Satan puts the fear in us.
But Christ takes away our fear and enables us to experience His
power and strength.

2 Corinthians 12:10 KJV
Therefore I take pleasure in infirmities, in reproaches, in necessities,
in persecutions, in distresses for Christ's sake: for when I am weak,
then am I strong.

October 19

Do not let fear rule over you,
And do not let your feelings put you down:
Let Christ be your strength to pull yourself together.

Philippians 4:13 KJV
I can do all things through Christ which strengtheneth me.

October 20

Difficulty and pain can help us grow;
Be thankful for the growing process.

1 Corinthians 15:57 KJV
But thanks be to God, which giveth us the victory through our
Lord Jesus Christ.

October 21

Trials come and go,
But our faith remains.
Our faith becomes stronger with every trial,
That we can testify God's faithfulness to others.

Psalm 89:1 KJV
I will sing of the mercies of the Lord (God) for ever: with my mouth
will I make known Thy faithfulness to all generations.

October 22

~◎ ◎~

God is faithful—lean on Him for protection and provision in your life.

Matthew 6:26 KJV
(Jesus said,)
Behold the fowls of the air: for they sow not, neither do they reap, nor gather into barns; yet your heavenly Father (God) feedeth them. Are ye not much better than they?

October 23

In Christ you can find healing.
He gives you peace and hope.
Believe in Him and be healed!

Isaiah 53:4–5 KJV
Surely He (Christ) hath borne our griefs, and carried our sorrows:
yet we did esteem Him stricken, smitten of God, and afflicted.
But He was wounded for our transgressions, He was bruised for our
iniquities: the chastisement of our peace was upon Him; and with
His stripes we are healed.

October 24

A thankful heart brings about a healthy soul and body.

Proverbs 15:13 KJV
A merry heart maketh a cheerful countenance: but by sorrow of the heart the spirit is broken.

October 25

Do not hold tight to your loved ones and worldly things, and drown yourselves in worries:
All these are not burdens from God.

Mark 4:19 KJV
(Jesus said,)
The cares of this world, and the deceitfulness of riches, and the lusts of other things entering in, choke the word, and it becometh unfruitful.

October 26

How can you hold on to God's hands when your hands are holding onto too many things of the world?

Let go of your worldly worries and hold on to God with your emptied hands, and trusting Him to take care of you.

Matthew 11:28 KJV
(Jesus said,)
Come unto Me, all ye that labour and are heavy laden, and I will give you rest.

October 27

Being rich or poor can challenge one's sinful nature;
Humble yourself before God regardless of your circumstances.

Proverbs 30:8–9 KJV
Remove far from me vanity and lies: give me neither poverty nor riches; feed me with food convenient for me:
Lest I be full, and deny Thee, and say, Who is the Lord? or lest I be poor, and steal, and take the name of my God in vain.

October 28

Every morning,
Whether rich or poor, we ought to give thanks to God for life and hope.

Psalm 150:6 KJV
Let every thing that hath breath praise the Lord (God). Praise ye the Lord.

October 29

Happiness is priceless and has no price tag on it.

Romans 4:7–8 KJV
Blessed are they whose iniquities are forgiven, and whose sins are covered.
Blessed is the man to whom the Lord (God) will not impute sin.

October 30

～◎ ◎～

God takes pleasure in a faithful child with a grateful heart.

Psalm 105:1 KJV
O give thanks unto the Lord (God); call upon His name: make known His deeds among the people.

October 31

Thank You for family and friends.
Thank You for good and bad times.
Thank You for the sun and the rain.
Thank You for the sowing and harvest seasons.
Thank You for times of enduring and healing.
Thank You for the waiting times and not rushing through life.
Thank You for peace today and hope for tomorrow.
And most of all,
THANKS IMMENSELY HEAVENLY FATHER (GOD) FOR
YOUR LOVE.

Psalm 107:8 KJV
Oh that men would praise the Lord (God) for His goodness, and
for His wonderful works to the children of men!

November 1

Judgment is God's job.
Our job is to love one another.

Romans 3:10–12, 22 KJV
There is none righteous, no, not one:
There is none that understandeth, there is none that seeketh after God.
They are all gone out of the way, they are together become unprofitable; there is none that doeth good, no, not one.
The righteousness of God which is by faith of Jesus Christ unto all and upon all them that believe: for there is no difference.

November 2

The scales of the world weigh us by what we deserve;
The grace of God tips the scales in favor of giving us what we do not deserve.

Romans 4:4–5 KJV
Now to him that worketh is the reward not reckoned of grace, but of debt.
But to him that worketh not, but believeth on Him (God) that justifieth the ungodly, his faith is counted for righteousness.

November 3

No one is perfect.
Not one is righteous.

Romans 3:23 KJV
For all have sinned, and come short of the glory of God.

November 4

See our flaws through others' eyes
And ask God to remove our flaws and renew us.

Matthew 7:3–5 KJV
(Jesus said,)
Why beholdest thou the mote that is in thy brother's eye, but considerest not the beam that is in thine own eye?
Or how wilt thou say to thy brother, Let me pull out the mote out of thine eye; and, behold, a beam is in thine own eye?
Thou hypocrite, first cast out the beam out of thine own eye; and then shalt thou see clearly to cast out the mote out of thy brother's eye.

November 5

Intentionally or unintentionally,
Sometimes people hurt us,
And at times we hurt others:
This is all due to our sinful nature.

Romans 12:17–18 KJV
Recompense to no man evil for evil. Provide things honest in the sight of all men.
If it be possible, as much as lieth in you, live peaceably with all men.

November 6

⁂

Through the power of our Lord Jesus Christ,
We learn to forgive others and ourselves.

Matthew 6:14–15 KJV
(Jesus said,)
For if ye forgive men their trespasses, your heavenly Father (God)
will also forgive you:
But if ye forgive not men their trespasses, neither will your Father
forgive your trespasses.

November 7

When you put the needs of others above your own,
You will experience great joy within yourself.

Hebrews 13:16 KJV
But to do good and to communicate forget not: for with such sacrifices God is well pleased.

November 8

Do not hold grudges and imprison yourself;
You are hurting yourself and your loved ones.

Romans 12:21 KJV
Be not overcome of evil, but overcome evil with good.

November 9

Turn grudges into forgiveness
And it will set you free to receive God's blessings.

1 Peter 3:9 NKJV
Not returning evil for evil or reviling for reviling, but on the contrary blessing, knowing that you were called to this, that you may inherit a blessing.

November 10

Bless yourself with a heart of forgiveness.
Holding grudges only destroys yourself.

Luke 11:4 KJV
(Jesus said,)
Forgive us our sins; for we also forgive every one that is indebted to
us. And lead us not into temptation; but deliver us from evil.

November 11

Retaliating is easy;
It comes naturally with us.
Forgiving is hard;
It comes through faith in Christ.

Ephesians 4:32 KJV
Be ye kind one to another, tenderhearted, forgiving one another, even as God for Christ's sake hath forgiven you.

November 12

⁊⊚ ⊙⊱

Look beyond defending yourself and forgive your offender,
And it will bring peace into a relationship.

Proverbs 18:21 KJV
Death and life are in the power of the tongue: and they that love it
shall eat the fruit thereof.

November 13

Do not attack one another with words.
Follow Jesus' example,
Let the righteous God be the judge.

Romans 12:19 KJV
Avenge not yourselves, but rather give place unto wrath: for it is written, Vengeance is mine; I will repay, saith the Lord (God).

November 14

※◎ ◎※

Satan cannot fight God one on one,
Thus he deceives us and uses our weaknesses against God.
Sometimes we feel sad and lonely,
But we are not alone;
For when we are weak, we are strong in the grace of God.

Jude 1:24 KJV
Now unto Him (God) that is able to keep you from falling, and to present you faultless before the presence of His glory with exceeding joy.

November 15

Without Jesus, we are powerless.
With Jesus who has already won the battle with Satan,
All we need to do is trust and rely on Jesus;
And we can defeat Satan whenever he attacks us.

Romans 16:20 KJV
The God of peace shall bruise Satan under your feet shortly. The grace of our Lord Jesus Christ be with you. Amen.

November 16

―――――――――――――――――――――

Fear hinders faith;
Trust ignites confidence.

2 Timothy 1:7 KJV
For God hath not given us the spirit of fear; but of power, and of love, and of a sound mind.

November 17

When we are faced with life's challenges,
Courage and the absence of fear are two different things.

Joshua 1:9b KJV
Be strong and of a good courage; be not afraid, neither be thou dismayed: for the Lord thy God is with thee whithersoever thou goest.

November 18

Stand firm in the truth of the gospel.
Hold on to your faith.
Embrace the hope in Christ.

Colossians 1:21–23 KJV
You, that were sometime alienated and enemies in your mind by wicked works, yet now hath He (God) reconciled
In the body of His (Christ's) flesh through death, to present you holy and unblameable and unreproveable in His sight:
If ye continue in the faith grounded and settled, and be not moved away from the hope of the gospel, which ye have heard, and which was preached to every creature which is under heaven.

November 19

Injustice in life is when the righteous suffers and the wicked goes unpunished.
Do not fret, nor be angry or jealous.
Instead, trust in God, be still, and patient;
And continue to live a godly life for God will ultimately bring justice.

Proverbs 10:28 KJV
The hope of the righteous shall be gladness: but the expectation of the wicked shall perish.

November 20

Suffering and injustice in life do not always come to resolution; Christ will reveal to us these mysteries in His glorious coming.

Romans 8:18 KJV
For I reckon that the sufferings of this present time are not worthy to be compared with the glory which shall be revealed in us.

November 21

God allows us to go through trials.
Trials can be our wake up calls.
Suffering redirects and sharpens our focus.

Revelation 3:1b–3a KJV
I (Christ) know thy works, that thou hast a name that thou livest, and art dead.
Be watchful, and strengthen the things which remain, that are ready to die: for I have not found thy works perfect before God.
Remember therefore how thou hast received and heard, and hold fast, and repent.

November 22

In all things,
Natural or man-made,
God is in control.

1 Corinthians 15:28 KJV
When all things shall be subdued unto Him (God), then shall the Son (Jesus) also Himself be subject unto Him that put all things under Him, that God may be all in all.

November 23

Your life may be a mess,
But Jesus can bring real change to you and the people around you.

Mark 9:23 KJV
(Jesus said,)
If thou canst believe, all things are possible to him that believeth.

November 24

Do not sell your soul to Satan for the powers of the world and become a slave to the flesh.

Instead, be a slave to Christ who gave His life as a ransom for your freedom.

Romans 6:22 KJV
But now being made free from sin, and become servants to God, ye have your fruit unto holiness, and the end everlasting life.

November 25

Do not follow the world's desires which lead to corruption,
But submit to God which leads to righteousness.

2 Peter 1:4 KJV
Whereby are given unto us exceeding great and precious promises:
that by these ye might be partakers of the divine nature, having
escaped the corruption that is in the world through lust.

November 26

A repentant heart pleases God;
It is one that is awaiting for the return of Christ to be with Him in
His glory.

Ezekiel 18:32 KJV
For I have no pleasure in the death of him that dieth, saith the Lord
God: wherefore turn yourselves, and live ye.

November 27

֍ ֍

A heart full of worldly desires
Will lead to wickedness and death.
Ask God for a new heart fills with His desire;
It will lead to a blessed and eternal life.

Ezekiel 18:30 KJV
Therefore I will judge you ... every one according to his ways, saith the Lord God. Repent, and turn yourselves from all your transgressions; so iniquity shall not be your ruin.

November 28

This world cannot give us real change and sure hope;
Real change and sure hope can only be found in Christ.

Psalm 25:6–7 KJV
Remember, O Lord (God),
Thy tender mercies and Thy lovingkindnesses; for they have been
ever of old.
Remember not the sins of my youth, nor my transgressions:
according to Thy mercy remember Thou me for Thy goodness'
sake, O Lord.

November 29

Love earthly things is human.
Love heavenly things is saint.

Colossians 1:26–27 KJV
Even the mystery which hath been hid from ages and from generations, but now is made manifest to His (God's) saints:
To whom God would make known what is the riches of the glory of this mystery among the Gentiles; which is Christ in you, the hope of glory.

November 30

Obey the teachings of the Bible,
And value what God values.

Acts 13:22b KJV
A man after Mine (God's) own heart, which shall fulfil all My will.

December 1

As you look back,
Count not your losses but your blessings.

Ecclesiastes 3:11–12 KJV
He (God) hath made every thing beautiful in His time: also He hath set the world in their heart, so that no man can find out the work that God maketh from the beginning to the end.
I know that there is no good in them, but for a man to rejoice, and to do good in his life.

December 2

In life,
When things go wrong, we often blame God;
But when things are right, we seldom praise Him.

Romans 8:38–39 KJV
For I am persuaded, that neither death, nor life, nor angels, nor principalities, nor powers, nor things present, nor things to come, Nor height, nor depth, nor any other creature, shall be able to separate us from the love of God, which is in Christ Jesus our Lord.

December 3

❧ ❧

What the world sees as failure,
God sees as a journey to success.

Joshua 1:8 KJV
This book of the law shall not depart out of thy mouth; but thou
shalt meditate therein day and night, that thou mayest observe to do
according to all that is written therein: for then thou shalt make thy
way prosperous, and then thou shalt have good success.

December 4

‿❦ ❧‿

God gives us the power and confidence to challenge the norm in this world.

1 John 5:1a, 4 KJV
Whosoever believeth that Jesus is the Christ is born of God ...
For whatsoever is born of God overcometh the world: and this is the victory that overcometh the world, even our faith.

December 5

Be content and happy despite your circumstances;
You cannot do this on your own,
Only through Christ who gives you strength.

Acts 16:31 KJV
Believe on the Lord Jesus Christ, and thou shalt be saved, and thy house.

December 6

Establish a genuine relationship with Christ,
And it will bring you true happiness and inner peace.

John 14:21 KJV
(Jesus said,)
He that hath My commandments, and keepeth them, he it is that
loveth Me: and he that loveth Me shall be loved of My Father (God),
and I will love him, and will manifest Myself to him.

December 7

─── ⁊◉ ◎℘ ───

Life goes through many stages.
Give yourself hope and purpose in every stage you are in.

Jeremiah 29:11 KJV
For I know the thoughts that I think toward you, saith the Lord
(God), thoughts of peace, and not of evil, to give you an expected end.

December 8

Life has its ups and downs.
In all situations,
Wait on God—always let Him go before you.

Psalm 27:14 KJV
Wait on the Lord (God): be of good courage, and He shall strengthen
thine heart: wait, I say, on the Lord.

December 9

When one door closes,
God opens another.

Revelation 3:8 KJV
(Jesus said,)
I know thy works: behold, I have set before thee an open door, and
no man can shut it: for thou hast a little strength, and hast kept My
word, and hast not denied My name.

December 10

〜◎ ◎〜

Put your confidence in the Almighty God.
We are stronger than we think.
There is nothing we face bigger than our God.

Psalm 50:1 KJV
The mighty God, even the Lord, hath spoken, and called the earth
from the rising of the sun unto the going down thereof.

Luke 1:37 KJV
For with God nothing shall be impossible.

December 11

God has given us conscience to guide our actions.
He has also given us the Holy Spirit to guide us as followers of
Christ.

Acts 24:16 KJV
Herein do I exercise myself, to have always a conscience void to
offence toward God, and toward men.

Romans 9:1 KJV
I say the truth in Christ, I lie not, my conscience also bearing me
witness in the Holy Ghost (Spirit).

December 12

Satan will continue to deceive and mislead us.
We must dwell in God's Word to resist the devil.

Psalm 119:11 KJV
Thy (God's) word have I hid in mine heart, that I might not sin against Thee.

December 13

Satan's power is limited.
God's Word can overpower the devil.

Ephesians 6:10–11 KJV
Be strong in the Lord, and in the power of His might.
Put on the whole armour of God, that ye may be able to stand against the wiles of the devil.

December 14

God's Word gives us wisdom, strength, and hope.

Psalm 119:105 KJV
Thy (God's) word is a lamp unto my feet, and a light unto my path.

December 15

Trust in yourself leads you closer to the world;
Trust in Christ leads you closer to God.

1 Corinthians 2:5 KJV
That your faith should not stand in the wisdom of men, but in the
power of God.

December 16

Turn away from the lies of Satan and the wickedness of the world. Turn to the truth of the Lord God and the righteousness of Jesus Christ.

Psalm 97:10–11 KJV
Ye that love the Lord (God), hate evil: He preserveth the souls of His saints; He delivereth them out of the hand of the wicked.
Light is sown for the righteous, and gladness for the upright in heart.

December 17

Accepting Jesus is easy;
Living for Jesus is not.

Matthew 16:24 KJV
(Jesus said,)
If any man will come after Me, let him deny himself, and take up his cross, and follow Me.

December 18

There are many churches but only one Head.
Christ is the Head of all churches on earth.

1 Peter 5:4 KJV
When the chief Shepherd (Jesus Christ) shall appear, ye shall receive
a crown of glory that fadeth not away.

December 19

Do not follow false leaders of the world;
Instead, follow God-fearing leaders.

Proverbs 12:26 NKJV
The righteous should choose his friends carefully,
For the way of the wicked leads them astray.

December 20

When the crowd drift away from the teachings of the Bible,
Do not follow them blindly, choose good over evil.

Psalm 119:74 KJV
They that fear Thee (God) will be glad when they see me; because
I have hoped in Thy word.

December 21

Do not compromise your faith because of cultures and traditions. Seek not the approval of human beings but God's approval alone.

Psalm 101:2–3 NKJV
I will behave wisely in a perfect way.
…
I will walk within my house with a perfect heart.
I will set nothing wicked before my eyes:
I hate the work of those who fall away;
It shall not cling to me.

December 22

We fall into temptations when we conform to the world. Trust in God and follow Jesus to live a victorious life.

Psalm 119:33–37 KJV

Teach me, O Lord (God), the way of Thy statutes; and I shall keep it unto the end.

Give me understanding, and I shall keep Thy law; yea, I shall observe it with my whole heart.

Make me to go in the path of Thy commandments; for therein do I delight.

Incline my heart unto Thy testimonies, and not to covetousness.

Turn away mine eyes from beholding vanity; and quicken Thou me in Thy way.

December 23

Commit to walk with the Lord Jesus Christ;
Never yield to the pressure of the world.

2 Thessalonians 3:5 KJV
The Lord (Jesus) direct your hearts into the love of God, and into
the patient waiting for Christ.

December 24

The culture around us often changes to conform to the world.
Stand firm in your faith to resist the ill trends:
Stand apart, do not go with the evils of the world.

Romans 12:2 KJV
Be not conformed to this world: but be ye transformed by the renewing of your mind, that ye may prove what is that good, and acceptable, and perfect, will of God.

December 25

Change is good only when it does not make you wander away from God's teachings.
Always follow the Holy Spirit's guidance and wait for God's timing to change.

Psalm 1:1–2 KJV
Blessed is the man that walketh not in the counsel of the ungodly, nor standeth in the way of sinners, nor sitteth in the seat of the scornful.
But his delight is in the law of the Lord (God); and in His law doth he meditate day and night.

December 26

Waiting is not idling.
Waiting is entrusting matters into God's hands.

Psalm 37:3–4 NKJV
Trust in the Lord (God), and do good;
Dwell in the land, and feed on His faithfulness.
Delight yourself also in the Lord:
And He shall give you the desires of your heart.

December 27

❧ ✦ ☙

Throw away your pride and self-reliance.
Put on Christ's humility and rely on God.

Psalm 131:1, 3 KJV
Lord (God), my heart is not haughty, nor mine eyes lofty: neither
do I exercise myself in great matters, or in things too high for me.
… Hope in the Lord from henceforth and for ever.

December 28

God's timing and His ways may be different from what we hope for; Keep trusting His authority and be faithful, and He will reward you.

1 Peter 5:6 KJV
Humble yourselves therefore under the mighty hand of God, that He may exalt you in due time.

December 29

Death, once done, cannot be undone.
But if we are still living,
It's never too late for anything.
The key in life is love, forgiveness, and hope.

Matthew 28:18–20 KJV
(Jesus said,)
All power is given unto Me in heaven and in earth.
Go ye therefore, and teach all nations, baptizing them in the name
of the Father (God), and of the Son (Jesus), and of the Holy Ghost
(Spirit):
Teaching them to observe all things whatsoever I have commanded
you: and, lo, I am with you always, even unto the end of the world.
Amen.

December 30

Today till eternity,
Christ is our sanctuary, our salvation, and our hope.

Hebrews 10:35–36 KJV
Cast not away therefore your confidence, which hath great
recompence of reward.
For ye have need of patience, that, after ye have done the will of
God, ye might receive the promise.

December 31

❧ ◖◗

As we end the year,
Remember Jesus has already overcome the world;
Therefore, always be on His side and share His victory.

John 16:33b KJV
(Jesus said,)
In Me ye might have peace. In the world ye shall have tribulation:
but be of good cheer; I have overcome the world.

As you follow through each day of this book, continue to mediate on the Scripture and keep God's Word in your heart, so to draw yourself even closer to Him in your everyday life.

Made in the USA
Lexington, KY
26 August 2018